David Hey

The Making of South Yorkshire

Moorland Publishing

British Library Cataloguing in Publication Data
Hey, David
    The Making of South Yorkshire.
    1. South Yorkshire, Eng. — History
    I. Title
    942.8'2   DA670.S66
    ISBN 0-903485-44-3

For A.K.Clayton
Local Historian

ISBN 0 903485 44 3

Photoset by Advertiser
Printers Ltd, Newton Abbot
and printed in Great Britain by
Dotesios (Printers) Ltd,
Bradford-on-Avon, Wiltshire for
Moorland Publishing Company
P.O. Box 2, 9-11 Station Street,
Ashbourne, Derbyshire,
DE6 1DZ.

Contents

Preface

It is commonly believed that South Yorkshire had no history worth speaking of before the Industrial Revolution — that the area was of little importance, if not backward, before the iron and steelworks were established and coal mining was developed on a large scale. Everyone knows that Conisbrough castle, Roche abbey and a few other places are well worth a visit, but it is often felt that history is something that happened somewhere else and that one must travel to other parts of Yorkshire or across the county boundary into Derbyshire or Lincolnshire to find historic buildings and earthworks of real worth and interest. The aim of this book is to show that such a view is mistaken. It deliberately stops well before the Industrial Revolution in order to demonstrate how much the present landscape has been moulded by the ancient past and to show what a wealth of material survives throughout the county.

The book is written for the interested amateur. It is concerned with the history of our everyday surroundings, with the way that places and institutions have come to be what they are. Our knowledge of the early history of the county has been deepened in recent years by excavations, aerial photography, place-name analysis, the study of vernacular architecture, fieldwork, and research amongst the vast collections of documents that have become available in local and national record offices, but much of this new work is known only to a few specialists. A general survey, written in non-technical language, is needed to bring the layman up to date.

New research is constantly altering the picture. At the time of writing, excavations are taking place at Rockley furnace and Warmsworth church, the remaining part of the College of Jesus at Rotherham is being surveyed systematically, more aerial photography is planned, and new discoveries through fieldwork and documentary research are continually surprising us all. Nowhere has the traditional picture been altered more than in the field of prehistory. So many new sites have been discovered through aerial photography in the last few years and so much re-assessment needs to be done that it has been felt wise in the present work to avoid a detailed discussion of the pre-Roman period and to start when written records, and thus history proper, began.

Division of Continuing Education, University of Sheffield.

4

Acknowledgements

Of the many friends who have discussed local history and archaeology with me and who have accompanied me to sites and record offices, I particularly wish to thank Malcolm Dolby (who took several of the photographs), John Magilton (who also drew the map of medieval Doncaster), Derek Holland, Paul Buckland, Arthur Clayton, Gerald Davies, Ted Spencer and Peter Ryder. Moreover, my former colleague in the Department of English Local History at the University of Leicester, Charles Phythian-Adams, has helped me to understand the county's early history in a national context. Needless to say each of these friends has views that do not always coincide with those expressed here. I am also grateful to Richard Bird, who took the bulk of the photographs and to Pauline Beswick who provided photographs from the collection at Sheffield City Museum.

The foundation of the county's historical studies is Joseph Hunter's monumental history of South Yorkshire, published in two volumes in 1828 and 1831. My indebtedness to Hunter and the numerous local historians who followed him will be obvious. We are also fortunate in having, at more recent times, A.H. Smith's volumes for the English Place-Name Society and Sir Nikolaus Pevsner's handbook on the West Riding's major buildings; they form the essential basis of any work on early local history. A list of the more useful books and articles and documentary sources is printed at the end of this volume. I have also been helped by archivists and museum officials and have benefited greatly from regular contacts with extramural and WEA class members throughout the county. Finally, I wish to thank the many people who have allowed me to walk over their property, to inspect their houses and outbuildings and even to climb into their attics. Their pride in their historic buildings is an abiding memory and one that augurs well for the preservation of our local heritage. But note that many of the sites mentioned in the text are on private land, and permission of the owner must be obtained before visiting.

The author and publisher would also like to thank the following for the use of illustrations: R.H. Bird; 4, 7, 8, 10, 13-15, 19, 21, 24, 26, 27, 29, 31, 33-7, 39, 40, 42-7, 49-51, 56-8, 61, 63-70; Director of Aerial Photography, University of Cambridge: 20, 62; M. Dolby and Doncaster Museums: 3, 18, 22, 41, 52; Meridian Airways Ltd: 32; J.R. Magilton of Doncaster Museum: 23; Sheffield City Libraries: 38; Sheffield City Museums: 53-5, 59, 60.

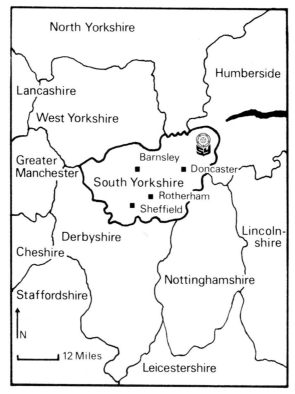

South Yorkshire in relation to its neighbouring counties.

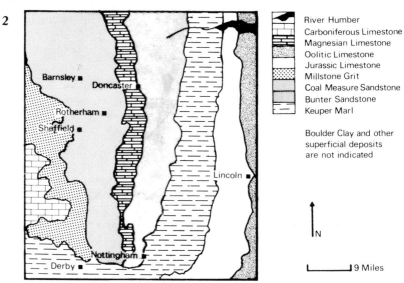

River Humber
Carboniferous Limestone
Magnesian Limestone
Oolitic Limestone
Jurassic Limestone
Millstone Grit
Coal Measure Sandstone
Bunter Sandstone
Keuper Marl

Boulder Clay and other
superficial deposits
are not indicated

N

9 Miles

The geology of the region.

Introduction

People spoke of 'South Yorkshire' long before the creation of the new county in 1974. It is true that the meaning attached to the term varied according to whether it was uttered in, say, the Dearne valley or in the rural villages well away from the coalmines, nevertheless there was a widespread feeling that this part of Yorkshire was somewhat different in its scenery, its occupations, and even in its pastimes and speech from the clothing district of the West Riding, the Dales or the plains of the Vale of York. Nor was this mere sentiment, for South Yorkshire did have some administrative unity in the earliest recorded periods of its history. In Anglo-Saxon times it lay upon the southern border of the kingdom of Northumbria and contained semi-independent estates such as Hallamshire and the fee of Conisbrough. This historic frontier is still followed for many miles by the present county boundary, except where it has been altered in the twentieth century to take account of building developments south of Sheffield. The diocese of York shared the same boundary, and the present county is not radically different from the medieval division of the diocese known as the deanery of Doncaster. Some parishes to the north have been lost, for the original boundary was the River Went, and there have been minor additions to the south, but the county is more or less the same district as that which Joseph Hunter wrote about in 1828 under the title, *South Yorkshire: The History and Topography of the Deanery of Doncaster.*

But despite this administrative unity, pre-industrial South Yorkshire was a region of great contrasts where it was possible in a journey of only 30 miles from west to east to pass through some of the most varied scenery in Britain. Today, the spoil heaps and winding gear, the factories and massive housing developments have obscured the great variety of landscapes and the diversity of forms of local community that were such a feature of the area before the reign of Queen Victoria. In a few places this sense of contrast can still be experienced, notably when standing on the ramparts of the Iron Age fort at Wincobank, with the hills and woods to the rear, looking down into the valley of the River Don between Sheffield and Rotherham at one of the largest industrial complexes in the country; or when a sudden climb on the road from Barnsley to Doncaster takes the traveller out of the coalfield at Goldthorpe up the Magnesian Limestone escarpment to a world of trim estate villages at Hickleton, High Melton and Hooton Pagnell; or again, when a short walk from the pit village of

Hoyland Common leads to the almost deserted site of Tankersley, with its ancient parish church, moated farm and rectory, medieval deer park and ruined Elizabethan hall. But in general the contrasts are less sharp than they were, and the old patterns of settlement and economy have been broken down by the effects of industrialisation.

In the western part of the county the rocks of the Millstone Grit series meet the sandstones, shales and clays of the older sections of the Coal-Measures to form the distinctive personality of the Pennines. Farmsteads and cottages, churches and chapels, workshops and mills, cowsheds and barns are all shaped from solid sandstone blocks, from stones mellowed with lichen or moss, light-grey stones whose grains of sand glitter in the sun, stones tinted with rust near the outcrops of ironstone, and stones soaked with soot in the towns or blackened by natural weathering in the countryside. Strangers remember above all the miles upon miles of stark, uncompromising walls that do not blend with the landscape but which are an essential part of its appeal. On a summer's evening the view from a high point such as Hartcliff Hill, near Penistone, some 1,150 feet above sea level, needs no sense of history to please the eye. But the pleasures of colour and form are deeply enriched by the knowledge that this landscape has been moulded by man over a period of many centuries. Prehistoric tools have been found on the moors, the outline of an Iron Age earthwork can be traced on a spur above Langsett, many of the farmsteads and hamlets are on sites that were first settled in the early medieval period, and the moorland track that climbs up the steep hill at Hartcliff is an immemorial highway that was once well trodden by the packhorses of the Cheshire salt traders. The gentle curve of the Sheffield to Manchester railway and the appealing calm of the reservoirs, set amongst bilberries and heather at Langsett and Midhope, demonstrate how well modern man has added to the natural beauty of the countryside. The working life of the small collieries and quarries is now over, and here industry has left few of the scars that disfigure so much of the rest of the county.

To the east of the Pennines thick woods once covered much of the Coal-Measure sandstones, and the ancient settlement pattern was one of scattered farms and hamlets in wooded clearances with a few villages in the river valleys. The hills, streams and woods provided an attractive setting for these small communities, and when Arthur Young visited the area in 1769 he wrote, 'The country between Sheffield and Barnsley is fine; it abounds with the beauties of landscape.' However, here were outcrops of the famous Barnsley and Silkstone beds of coal and of thinner seams such as at Parkgate and the Thorncliffe, so it was naturally in this part of South Yorkshire that the earliest industrial changes took place. In 1830, two generations after Young's journey, William Cobbett travelled along the same road and noted, 'All the way along from Leeds to Sheffield it is coal and iron, and iron and coal.' By the end of the nineteenth century the district had been transformed, and between the towns the characteristic form of settlement became the pit village, unlovely to look at, but justly renowned for the warmth of its social life and the strength of its community feeling.

In recent times the old deposits have been exhausted and the centre of the coalfield has moved from Barnsley to Doncaster, where deeper pits have been sunk to the seams as they dip towards the east. Between these two towns lies a rich agricultural region. Many of the small villages in the eastern part of the sandstone area were purely agricultural until the Victorian era, and a few remain so today. Further east, a narrow band of Magnesian Limestone, never more than five miles wide, overlies the coal, and to the south of Doncaster a few square miles of sandy soils have never been surrendered to industry. Together they form a welcome stretch of countryside amidst the collieries. Not all of the old villages have escaped, for Adwick le Street, Conisbrough, Dinnington and Maltby have been altered radically by coal mining, but elsewhere great lords or village squires have preserved the rural nature of their ancient settlements. New Edlington is quite separate from the old parish centre, and at Hickleton and Frickley the colliery communities have been banished beyond the parish boundaries, out of sight from the lord's hall. This fertile region appears to have been the first part of the county to attract settlers, and aerial photographs have revealed an astonishing series of crop marks from the Romano-British period and the Iron Age. The historic differences between this district and the other parts of the county go right back to the origins of the settlements. Here were compact villages rather than hamlets and scattered farmsteads, here was arable land farmed on the open-field system instead of pasture closes and hill-meadows, and here the relatively dense population in early times meant that parishes were small like those in Midland England instead of huge, rambling territories with ill-defined boundaries as in the Pennines or the marshlands.

In the eastern part of the county the landscape is so utterly different in character from the west that it is hard to imagine that the Pennines are so near. Here is none of the romantic splendour of the hills, yet these miles upon miles of former fens, with vast expanses of sky above low horizons, have an appeal all of their own. Abraham de la Pryme, a descendant of the Dutch and Flemish settlers who came over with Cornelius Vermuyden upon the draining of Hatfield Chase in the 1620s, wrote of Hatfield at the close of the seventeenth century in a way that only a local person could.

It is situated upon a pleasant, fruitful and happy soil, neither too high nor too low, [nor] too subject to durt in winter, nor too troublesome in summer by reason of its dust; 'tis not too much exposed to winds, nor rendered unpleasant at any time by vapours or mists, but every thing conjoins in one to make it pleasant and neat. It stands in the midst of an almost round field, not disfigured by hills and dailes, perpetually green with corn in one part or other, and the pleasant oaks, and woody pastures and closes, which encompass this field and town round about, gives a most delectable prospect to the eye.

The coalmines that were sunk in this district at the beginning of the twentieth century, together with the housing estates that grew around them, have lessened the sense of contrast between the fens and the rest of the county, but even now, away from the collieries and the newer settlements, the affinities of the region are more with Lincolnshire or even with Holland than with the Millstone Grit country and the Coal-Measure sandstones in the west. On a sultry day when thunder threatens, when the silver birches shimmer and the sphagnum mosses glisten, the remarkable stillness of Thorne Waste and Hatfield Chase provides a memorable experience, as powerful in its appeal as the peace of the Pennines.

When standing alone on the banks of a sluggish fenland dyke or upon an ancient wizened head of Millstone on a moorland escarpment with only the peewits to disturb the solitude, it is hard to believe that not many miles away is so much industry, so many people. South Yorkshire has paid a heavy price for being in the vanguard of the Industrial Revolution, but the county has many attractions as well as its eyesores and its history is not just that of coal mining and the manufacture of iron and steel. To understand how our towns and villages acquired their present form and character it is often necessary to go back many centuries before the Industrial Revolution. Indeed, some places have stories that go back beyond the settlements of the Normans, Danes, Angles, Romans and Celts to prehistoric times.

Ideas about the prehistory of South Yorkshire have undergone a considerable change in recent years and it is now obvious that early man occupied much more of the county than was once believed. Few sites have been excavated and the tools and weapons that have been discovered so far have been mostly surface finds. This has given a misleading impression, for fieldwork has naturally been concentrated in those areas that have interested the comparatively few people who have been actively involved in local archaeology, and it is easier to discover evidence from uncultivated land than it is to recover anything from those parts of the county where centuries of building and of industrial or farming activities have obliterated most traces of early occupation. Aerial photography is now beginning to redress the balance, for even where earthworks and habitation sites have been ploughed flat they can produce crop-marks that can be seen from the air in favourable weather conditions. Though only a few tools have been found on the Magnesian Limestone and the eastern parts of the Coal-Measure sandstones, this central area yields the best crop marks, and photographs show that it was occupied successively over a very long period of time. Upon these light, fertile soils settled farming was first practised in South Yorkshire.

3

Crop marks that can be seen only from the air often preserve the ground plans of buildings that have long since vanished. This Romano-British enclosure at Marr is typical of the numerous early sites that have been discovered in the last few years in the central part of the county.

South Yorkshire lies across the boundary of the Highland and Lowland zones of Britain. The Highland zone has always been late in receiving new influences and slow to adapt to them, so the various prehistoric 'ages' merged quietly and old techniques continued in use long after their rejection in those parts of England that were open to new ideas from the Continent. Thus, Mesolithic flints and chert tools have been found in a Neolithic barrow at Crow Chin, near Moscar, and a flint arrowhead that would normally be associated with the the Neolithic period has been found in a Middle Bronze Age cremation urn in the Sheffield suburb of Crookes. Gradual rather than violent change is also the usual theme in later times.

Aerial photography and intensive fieldwork are beginning to show that large areas of the North Midlands were developed agriculturally before the coming of the Romans and that many Romano-British settlements may have been founded upon earlier sites. Parts of South Yorkshire were first cultivated at a much earlier period than was once supposed, and if the earthworks preserved in ancient woods at Edlington and Wombwell are anything to go by the local Iron Age farmers were obviously men of some substance. Of all the phases in the prehistory of South Yorkshire (which goes back to the hunter-fishermen of the Palaeolithic or Old Stone Age) the Iron Age is as yet the least understood, for in the absence of a recognisable pottery style the sites are notoriously difficult to interpret. Recent excavations at Dunsville, for instance, revealed the dimensions of an Iron Age farmstead but produced only two fragments of pottery. However, aerial photography has identified the characteristic ground plans of small farmsteads in the central part of the county and in the eastern lowlands, and pollen analysis on the Pennines suggests a less nomadic population and larger herds grazing the hills in summer.

The most obvious landscape features from the Iron Age are the communal hill forts, which were constructed with immense labour at various times from the sixth century BC to the first century AD. The strongest Iron Age fortress in South Yorkshire was that on Wincobank Hill, overlooking a strategic crossing of the River Don. Modern housing has come almost to the top of the hill, but the 2½ acre enclosure is still intact, protected by a double rampart and a bank constructed of earth over a dry-stone wall. Naturally, the ramparts are less imposing than they were and the ditches have been partly silted up, but the site is still impressive and the visitor is left in no doubt that the position was a commanding one. On the moors on the other side of Sheffield, well-known to hikers and to motorists heading for Hathersage, is Carl Wark, a fort that is smaller than Wincobank and one that defends a spur rather than the highest hill in the vicinity. The name suggests that the site was refortified in the Dark Ages that followed the retreat of the Romans, but the great walls and banks that supplemented the natural defences are probably Iron Age in origin. Even more puzzling are the small defensive earthworks that can still be recognised on promontories or hill-slopes at Canklow, Langsett, Scholes and Sutton Common, and which existed until recently at Roe Wood and Rough Birchworth. The small size and limited defensive nature of these earthworks suggest that they were associated with minor settlements, such as the Iron Age farmstead which once stood on Canklow Hill.

Very few obvious Iron Age features survive in the present landscape. Nevertheless, it is becoming clear that a great deal of land had been brought under the plough or cleared for stock-raising by the time that the Romans arrived and written records began.

4

The Iron Age fort at Wincobank defended the crossing of the River Don against invaders from the south. It checked the advance of the Romans and caused them to build their own fort on the other bank of the river at Temple-borough.

Romans, Angles and Vikings

The Romans

Forts The Romans did not try to conquer the North immediately but made peace with Cartimandua, queen of the federation of Celtic tribes known as the Brigantes. The history of the Roman period is much clearer than anything that went before because written sources are available for the first time and the great increase in military and economic activities has long attracted the interest of archaeologists. In 54 AD the Romans built a series of advanced forts at Derby, Templeborough and Castleford in order to support Cartimandua in her struggle with her former consort, Venutius. The fort at Templeborough stood on the southern bank of the River Don, almost opposite the Brigantian stronghold at Wincobank, but it now lies buried beneath the works of the British Steel Corporation. It covered about 6½ acres and was enclosed by a ditch and turf rampart. Eight hundred soldiers of the Fourth Cohort of Gauls, including about 240 cavalry men, were stationed here until 69 AD, when Venutius overthrew his queen and assumed control of the Brigantes. The Romans immediately advanced north, destroyed the hill forts, and defeated Venutius at Stanwick. A new phase of the military occupation now began and the Romans consolidated their position by moving the Ninth Legion from Lincoln to York. At Templeborough the old timber buildings were removed and a new fort was erected in local sandstone. When peace was secured, bath houses were constructed between the defences and the River Don, and an industrial annexe with a smithy and a glass furnace heated by coal was built to exploit the local resources.

The name Templeborough appears to have been an antiquarian invention, and in earlier times the site was simply called Brough, meaning a fort. The Roman name is not known, but there is no doubt that the other major fort in the county was referred to in Roman times as Danum. Our understanding of Roman Doncaster has increased enormously as the result of the excavations undertaken in the last few years, and much undoubtedly remains to be discovered. The fort established soon after 70AD was a large one of 9½ acres, with timber buildings and a cobbled road. The original ditch and rampart have been located near St George's church and a short by-road has been shown to have connected the fort to a few civilian houses alongside the main north-south highway. Upon the building of Hadrian's wall the fort was abandoned, but it was rebuilt on a smaller scale shortly before 160AD. This new military centre covered 5.85 acres and was surrounded by an eight-foot wide defensive wall built of stones which appear to have been quarried a few miles to the west. A civil settlement lay to the south and west of the fort, and finds include not only a coin hoard and pieces of pottery and glass, but the stone image of a goddess and a stone column from the granaries. The fort was regarrisoned during the late third or fourth century and coin evidence shows that it was occupied until at least 390. Danum occupied a key point, for not only was it sited at a major crossing of the River Don, which is still used to this day, it was also the limit of inland navigation for coastal vessels. At the heart of modern Doncaster is one of the county's most historic sites, a centre of great importance for a wide region, which was re-used time and time again by new settlers, but which is now ruthlessly sundered by a new road to enable traffic to hurry to the east. Fortunately, excavation schemes have been encouraged and are adding to our knowledge every year. During the long, hot summer of 1976 it became obvious that the civil settlement was much larger than was once believed, for excavations undertaken in St Sepulchre Gate revealed three parallel defensive ditches well beyond the fort. They appear to have been town defences of the late Roman period and show that Roman Doncaster was much more than just a fort controlling a key crossing of the River Don. Templeborough was never developed in the same way; its civil settlement was built ¾ mile to the south, near Brinsworth, and in the post-Roman period the fort was abandoned in favour of a new site at the other side of the confluence of the Don and the Rother.

Roads   Three minor forts along or near the highway from Lincoln to York have been discovered by aerial photography. A fourth-century fort, only ½ acre in size, was identified by the River Idle east of Bawtry, where it no doubt guarded the light craft which came this far up the river. Excavation finds had helped to date this fort, but in the dry summer of 1976 crop marks showed that it was within a much larger and earlier fort. The highway to the north from Bawtry avoided the fens of Hatfield Chase by following the sandy ridge to the next fort, which defended the crossing of the River Torne at Rossington Bridge. The drainage of this area was considerably altered in the seventeenth century by Cornelius Vermuyden, so it is no longer possible to judge whether this too was an inland port; it would certainly have been a convenient export point for the very important potteries that have been discovered in this vicinity. Aerial photography has also revealed considerable evidence of Iron Age and Roman field systems in this area. From Rossington Bridge Roman roads continued north to the Don, at Danum and further down the river near Wheatley, where some kind of settlement has been located at the International Harvesters' Factory. Stretches of the latter road have been

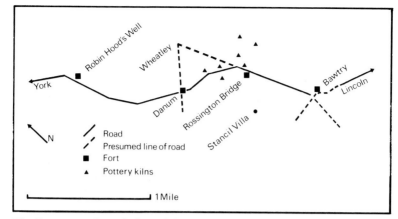

The Roman road north through Danum.

identified near Cantley and are marked on the Ordnance Survey map. The road has not been traced to the north of the Don, and it is possible that Wheatley also served as a river port. The other road entered Doncaster via the present racecourse and South Parade, headed for firm ground on the Magnesian Limestone at Adwick, and continued to the third known fort near Robin Hood's Well on the edge of the Forest of Barnsdale. There is little doubt that these forts were built immediately after the conquest of the Brigantes and that the road connecting them was constructed for military purposes. The later road long remained a prominent landmark and stretches of the raised agger and the ditch can still be traced along the lane between the Sun Inn and the Red House. The Anglo-Saxons described Roman roads as 'streets,' and like the famous road that now forms the basis of the A5, part of this highway was known as the Watling Street. As late as 1764 it was described in a Bentley glebe terrier as 'an old Roman way called the Street,' and the neighbouring village of Adwick le Street is so named to avoid confusion with Adwick upon Dearne.

According to a document of 1400 this highway was formerly known as the East Street, presumably to distinguish it from the prehistoric road adapted by the Romans as Ricknield Street. This ancient road survives in parts as country lanes that head northwards along the crest of the Magnesian Limestone as directly as the local topography allows. The whole of its course through South Yorkshire can be followed approximately on the Ordnance Survey map, for like the road through Danum it was chosen as a boundary by several ancient parishes in later times. Today, the minor road that separates the parish of Harthill from that of Thorpe Salvin is known as Packman Lane, but according to Joseph Hunter, writing in 1828, it was described in a Harthill terrier as 'an old Roman way, now called the Street.' Thomas Jefferys' map of Yorkshire (surveyed 1767-72) marks the hamlet of Streethouses at the point where

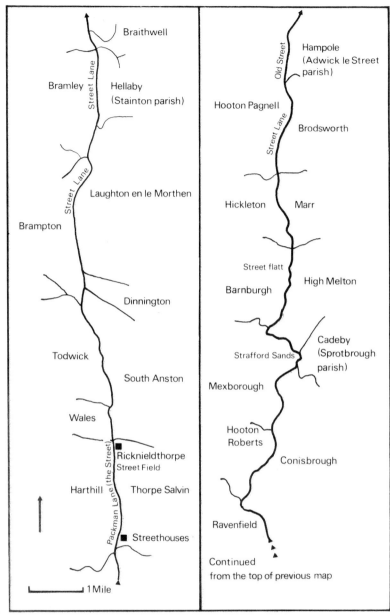

Braithwell

Bramley

Street Lane

Hellaby
(Stainton parish)

Laughton en le Morthen

Street Lane

Brampton

Dinnington

Todwick

South Anston

Wales

Ricknieldthorpe
Street Field

Packman Lane (the Street)

Harthill

Thorpe Salvin

Streethouses

1 Mile

Hampole
(Adwick le Street
parish)

Old Street

Hooton Pagnell

Brodsworth

Street Lane

Hickleton

Marr

Street flatt

Barnburgh

High Melton

Strafford Sands

Cadeby
(Sprotbrough
parish)

Mexborough

Hooton
Roberts

Conisbrough

Ravenfield

Continued
from the top of previous map

Ricknield Street as marked by ancient parish boundaries.

Packman Lane crosses the county boundary. Just to the north of Street
Field is the hamlet of West Thorpe, which in earlier times was known as
Ricknieldthorpe. Its original name points to the fact that during the
Roman period this highway formed one of the branches of the great

Ricknield Street that headed towards York. The Romans appear to have adapted it in the same manner as they used part of the prehistoric 'Jurassic Way' north of Stamford in the construction of Ermine Street. Further north, that part of the highway which separated Laughton from Brampton at Thurcroft, and Bramley from Hellaby, was also known as Street Lane, and the passage across the Ings where the Dearne and the Don meet east of Mexborough was called simply 'the street ford,' or in later times, Strafford Sands. Here were held the meetings of the wapentake of Strafforth during the years of Danish rule, though after the Norman conquest the name was changed to Strafforth and Tickhill and meetings were no longer held in the open air. Beyond the ford the route continues in a northerly direction and further street names are soon found upon it. A field in Barnburgh parish once had the suggestive name of Street-flatt; the lane that separates the parish of Hooton Pagnell from that of Brodsworth is known as Street Lane; and the highway is known as Old Street where it forms the boundary between Hooton and Hampole. Its antiquity is suggested by its character as a ridgeway along the limestone and by the prehistoric remains that have been found alongside it, notably the barrow that once stood at the junction of the three parishes of Barnburgh, High Melton and Marr, and the Iron Age field systems revealed by aerial photography.

The road that approached Templeborough from the south, possibly from Ricknield Street, has recently been located near Whiston, but attempts to fix a route north of the Don have so far been unsuccessful. Templeborough may have been linked with Wath upon Dearne (the name means a ford) and with Street Balk, a lane that heads north-north-east

7

Street Lane still serves as the parish boundary between Hooton Pagnell and Brodsworth. This prehistoric route through the central part of the county was adapted by the Romans and can still be traced by the place-names alongside it.

from Thurnscoe towards the two major streets described earlier. Another possibility is that a road went from Sheffield towards the hamlet of Street near Wentworth and on past Darfield (where three major coin hoards have been discovered) towards Street Lane in Little Houghton, but both these suggestions are based purely upon place-name evidence. The idea of a road from Wheatley and Danum to Templeborough has more tangible support, but as yet it is not known whether it continued further west. However, it is certain that a major east-west road through South Yorkshire passed to the south of these forts; coming from Lincoln via Littleborough (Notts) and crossing the Idle at Bawtry, it followed the line of the agger that is visible in the fields between Oldcotes and Firbeck, and crossed the River Rother at Catcliffe; it then entered Sheffield via the Cricket Inn Lane and proceeded along Sandygate, Lydgate Lane and the Long Causeway to the fort at Brough, near Hope, and so on to Chester. The economy of Roman South Yorkshire was more advanced than has been realised until recently, and in addition to the routes linking the forts it is likely that several minor roads of a civil rather than a military nature await discovery.

The Economy Once the frontier of Roman Britain had been pushed much further north both soldiers and natives were able to follow normal peacetime activities. Thus, a bronze diploma found at Stannington appears to have been the equivalent of discharge papers issued to an auxiliary soldier in 124AD, and a ditched site alongside the Ricknield Street at Kiveton Park has yielded pottery from a similar period, together with the remains of a corn-drying kiln and the bones of domesticated animals. The civil settlements near Danum and Templeborough have already been mentioned, and pollen analysis has shown that even on the edge of the Pennines corn was grown during the Roman period. Four miles south of Danum and two miles east of the fort at Rossington Bridge the rich farm lands encouraged some wealthy Roman, or possibly a prominent native who had accepted the inevitability of Roman rule, to lay out a villa. So impressive was this building that in later times the settlement acquired the name of Stancil, a corruption of 'stone-dwelling hall'. The medieval village that grew up around this villa was later deserted and this site which has still so much to tell us is now threatened with deep ploughing methods that would destroy it for ever.

More settlements undoubtedly await discovery, for coin hoards indicate that a certain amount of wealth was circulating throughout most of the present county. No less than 981 silver coins and 541 copper coins have been found at Darfield; nearly 2,000 coins were stored in two vases at Throapham; 1,200 coins were hoarded at Tickhill; 609 and 53 in two hoards at Edlington Wood, about 300 at Campsall, and 70 at Marr. Altogether, Roman coins have been found in about 60 different parts of the county, but it is surely significant that all the major hoards were discovered in the central part. Once again, this region appears as the one most favoured by early settlers.

Romano-British potsherds of various kinds have been found at several places within the county and a vast amount of ware has been recovered from six pottery sites to the south-east of Danum, most recently at Bessacarr. The most important site was at Cantley, where no less than forty-one kilns and an iron furnace have been excavated. Here was one of the largest Roman industrial complexes in the country, a major centre where the potters specialised in the production of coarse grey bowls, jars and dishes. Nearby at Rossington Bridge a wider range of wares was manufactured and some fine drinking vessels were sold as far north as lowland Scotland. They date from the second half of the second century to the mid-fourth century, and some of the earlier wares are stamped with the names of Sarrius (who is known to have worked also in Warwickshire) and of his partners, Secundua and Setebocius. This splendid collection of pots is now on display in Doncaster Museum, together with a reconstruction of a clay-built kiln.

In the west of the county industrial activity of a different kind is apparent from the discoveries of scores of beehive querns, which were used for grinding corn. Four Romano-British sites and the outlines of their field systems have been identified on the ridge near Grenoside (whose name means 'the quarry hill') and Wharncliffe ('the quern-cliff'). The querns were probably exported to many different parts of the country. Fieldwork and aerial photography in recent years have produced far more indications of human enterprise in this period than was ever thought possible. In recent months, for instance, Romano-British settlements have been identified in association with a round barrow at High Melton and early field systems have been located from the air at Sprotbrough. Typical 'Celtic fields' of up to two acres have been found near Rossington Bridge, between Hickleton and Marr, and on Smarson's Hill at Anston, where they are associated with numerous potsherds from the third and fourth centuries. At least three Romano-British sites have been discovered along the line of the proposed motorway between Wadworth and Hatfield, and not far away, in Edlington Wood, a Romano-British farmstead is known to have had three periods of occupation between the first and third centuries. The double ditch that runs in a straight line through the wood is likely to have been an ancient boundary.

Most of the evidence for early settlement no doubt lies buried beneath our towns and villages, for it is very likely that early man favoured many of the same places chosen by the Anglo-Saxons and their medieval successors. In the centre of Sheffield, and elsewhere, archaeological levels have been destroyed for ever, but other places still provide opportunities for future excavations. At the moment we can only speculate on, for instance, the possibility of Roman settlement at Conisbrough, which was ideally placed near where the Ricknield Street crossed the highway from Danum to Templeborough, not far from the important river crossing at Strafford Sands. So far only two Roman coins have been discovered upon the site of the Norman castle, but here and elsewhere archaeological investigations may one day change the picture.

2 The Anglo-Saxons

The Romans left Britain early in the fifth century and for over 200 years most of South Yorkshire was free from foreign invaders. Hardly anything is known about the county during this period and 'The Dark Ages' is still an apt description. At the moment South Yorkshire has little light to shed on the problem of possible continuity between the settlements of the Romans and the Anglo-Saxons. What has been established is that the Angles arrived here rather late and that the independent British kingdom of Elmet survived until the second or third decade of the seventh century. Edwin of Northumbria, who won his throne at a battle on the east bank of the River Idle in 616, finally conquered the Britons a few years later. In 633 he was killed by the allied forces of Penda of Mercia and Cadwallon, the British ruler of North Wales, at the battle of Hatfield. Local tradition claims that the site of the battle was at Slay Pits near the village of Hatfield, but the mass burials under the church at Cuckney and the place-name Edwinstowe suggest that the battle was fought in north Nottinghamshire, which was part of the great district known as Hatfield. It is just possible that the name Slay Pits commemorates the earlier battle of 616.

Despite this long period of independence relatively few place-names within the county are obviously Celtic in origin. Campsall's first element is a British personal name, and we still use the Celtic (or pre-Celtic) words for the rivers Dearne, Don, Dove and Rother. The Anglo-Saxons occasionally used British words for prominent features in the landscape and added an ending of their own; thus, Ecclesfield and Ecclesall refer to British churches, Penistone to the great ridge between the valley of the Don and the Little Don, and Rossington to a moor. Groups of natives who continued to farm land on the outskirts of Anglo-Saxon settlements were described by their folk names, and these are retained today in the village names of Wales and (possibly) Monk Bretton. But the rarity of Celtic survivals does not mean that large parts of the county were without settlers before the coming of the Anglo-Saxons, or that the Britons were all killed or forced to flee. Throughout England many names have changed and earlier names are sometimes hidden in present forms. The lack of documentary evidence for South Yorkshire before 1086 makes the task of the place-name scholar a peculiarly difficult one, but the archaeological evidence makes it quite clear that much of the county was settled before the arrival of the Anglo-Saxons. The framework of the estates established by the native Britons was preserved for centuries, and it is no longer possible to believe that these Celtic people were driven out by the invaders. The Anglo-Saxons were the new masters, but the Britons continued to farm their land as before.

After the battle of Hatfield Mercian Angles ruled over west Yorkshire as far north as Airedale, but when Penda was killed in battle in 654 the whole of Yorkshire reverted to Northumbrian rule. During the seventh century, therefore, Britons, Mercians and Northumbrians lived alongside each other in this frontier zone. The scarcity of early forms of Anglian place-names supports the view that their occupation of this region was late when compared with many other parts of the country. A few small pieces of pottery and the traces of a hut from the pagan period have been found at Danum, but it is likely that on the whole the Angles were already Christian by the time they arrived in the Christian kingdom of Elmet. The surviving place-names are of little help in determining the pattern of early Anglian settlement, for they do not contain folk names or personal names that are known to date from the earliest period. Recent research, however, has suggested that the ending *ham* was the usual name given to an original farmstead, especially if the name was combined with that of a river. South Yorkshire has only two *ham* settlements recorded in Domesday Book, and their fortunes in later times could hardly have been more varied. On the Magnesian Limestone, just off Ricknield Street in the parish of Hooton Pagnell, stand Bilham House Farm and Bilham Grange, where once stood a small medieval village, and way back in the seventh century the solitary farm of the settler Billa. By way of contrast, the other early settlement has been transformed into the modern industrial town of Rotherham. The place-name is undoubtedly early for it combines the *ham* element with a Celtic river name. The Angles preferred a new site a mile to the east of Templeborough, at the other side of the confluence of the Rother and the Don, near what remained a key communications centre until the M1 motorway provided an easier route across the Don. No doubt in early times primitive craft transported goods along both rivers.

Pasture land in the open spaces was described as *feld*, which in time became the place-name element *field*. Though this element is not usually regarded as an early feature it is interesting to find that it occurs in the names of several South Yorkshire settlements that became the centres of ancient parishes or other administrative units. Thus, in the south-west the territory known as Hallamshire had three components, namely Ecclesfield, Sheffield and Bradfield, and though Bradfield simply means the broad *feld*, the other two names are undoubtedly early; Sheffield takes its name from a river and is sited where a Roman road crossed the Sheaf near to its confluence with the Don, and Ecclesfield's name is derived from the British church which was still standing in the *feld* when the Angles first arrived. In the eastern part of the county Austerfield was the venue of an important church synod in 702 and the people of Hatfield were named as a distinct group in the eighth-century *Tribal Hidage,* and for centuries Hatfield was the recognised centre of the lowlands east of Doncaster. Darfield and Ravenfield, the other two *feld* settlements to be recorded in Domesday Book were also heads of ancient parishes, and at Darfield hoards of Roman coins have been discovered. After the Norman conquest *field* acquired a different meaning, something like its present sense, and in some parts of the country it simply meant a forest clearing, even in early phases of colonisation. But when the Angles penetrated Elmet they seem to have used *feld* to describe large areas of pasture that had already been cleared for stock-rearing. Evidence from West Yorkshire and North Derbyshire supports the view that in early times *feld* was attached to places of importance; Wakefield, Mirfield, Huddersfield, Chesterfield and Dronfield were each centres of considerable antiquity.

The two major Roman roads remained in use long after the collapse of the Empire and were such prominent landscape features in later times that long stretches were used as parish boundaries. As in other parts of England, the Anglo-Saxons did not settle alongside the old roads but sought refuge in secluded places half a mile or more away. The settlers also penetrated the river valleys in search of small spurs above the flood plain, ideally at points where the river could be crossed. Adwick upon Dearne, Bolton upon Dearne and Wath upon Dearne were founded in this manner and eventually became the heads of parishes. So did Darfield and Darton, a few miles upstream, but though each stands on a spur almost on the banks of the Dearne the name is apparently derived from deer. The lack of early documentary evidence is regrettable, but it is quite clear that not only the Dearne but the Don and Rother were used by settlers in search of suitable sites.

The Anglo-Saxons gradually abandoned their use of *ham* and spoke instead of *tons.* Both were applied originally to farmsteads, then to hamlets and eventually to villages. *Ton* was the usual choice in South Yorkshire and 39 widely scattered places with the *-ton* ending are recorded in Domesday Book. Sometimes *ton* was coupled with a personal name, as in Dinnington or Edlington, sometimes with a topographical feature, as in Clayton ('farmstead on the clay'), Hooton ('farmstead on the spur of land') or Stainton ('stone farmstead'). The next most popular choice was *ley,* which meant a woodland clearing and was coupled either with a personal name, as in Auckley, Barnsley, Tankersley or Wadsley, or with some peculiar local feature such as the bent grass in Bentley or the broom in Bramley. A further fifteen Domesday settlements had the ending *worth,* meaning an enclosure. Here again the names are widely distributed and are recorded in 1086 even in such inhospitable parts of the Pennines as Holdsworth, Ingbirchworth and Rough Birchworth must have been. *Worth* apparently became a popular element after the early stages of colonisation were complete, for only four heads of ancient parishes were named in this way. Extensive areas of moorland, marshland and woodland were uncultivated when the Danes arrived in the ninth century, But the Angles had already occupied most of the best sites and a considerable number of inferior ones.

The use of so many different personal names in the place-names of South Yorkshire implies a system of individual ownership within large estates. It is now clear from studies of other parts of the country that the people commemorated in our present place-names are rarely the original settlers but more usually later owners. No pre-Norman charters and only one Anglo-Scandinavian will survive for this region, so there is little firm evidence about early settlement, but it seems clear that most of our villages and some of our towns started as single farmsteads. However, in times of danger collective action was needed, and at some unknown period long before the Norman conquest what appears to have been an organised system of defence was constructed along or near the banks of the Don and the Dearne at Barnburgh, Conisbrough, Doncaster, Kexbrough, Masbrough, Mexborough, Sheffield, Sprotbrough, Stainborough and Worsbrough. The foundation dates of these forts are at present as mysterious as are those of the long ditches known as the Roman Rig and the Bar Dike, which may have been defensive in purpose but are most likely to have been boundaries between different tribes or peoples. The Bar Dike is 450 yards long and has a rampart on its southern side which in places is ten feet higher than the bottom of the ditch. It ends at two steep valleys and controls the north-south crossing of Broomhead Moor. A mile or so to the north a similar ditch runs parallel to the Bar Dike for ¾ mile along the top of the Ewden Beck valley. The so-called Roman Rig, which lies much further to the east, was described in 1693 as 'a cussen Dich there called Kempe Ditch.' Cussen is an archaic dialect word meaning cast-up, and

8

The ancient route over Bradfield and Broomhead moors is barred by this great trench known as Bar Dike. Its date is unknown but it probably goes back to the Dark Ages following the withdrawal of the Romans.

kempe means warrior. Several stretches of this ditch survive, but although sections have been excavated its date is not known. The bank on the southern side has been thrown-up rather than constructed, nevertheless there is uniformity of design throughout the ten miles from the Pennine foothills at Sheffield to the marshy ground near Mexborough and Kilnhurst. In the western part one ditch was considered satifactory, but on the gentler slopes further east it was thought necessary to construct two dykes roughly parallel to each other and about half a mile apart. They may be contemporary with the linear earthworks in West Yorkshire known as Becca Banks and may even guard the same territory. Like the great Wansdike and Offa's Dyke they apparently belong to the 'Dark Ages' that followed the collapse of the Roman Empire.

Some dialect forms and the use of words such as owler for alder and wang for meadow show that much of the Anglian settlement of this region was from the Midlands. Ickles, near Rotherham, is a Mercian place-name, and Warmsworth takes its name from Wermi, a Mercian settler. This peaceful colonisation may well have continued long after the Northumbrians regained military control. Soon however there were to be settlers of an altogether different kind.

3   The Scandinavians

Danish invaders arrived on the coast of Yorkshire in 865. Halfdene's army made their headquarters in York, but the invasion of South Yorkshire seems to have been made by the army that Guthrum had led into the East Midlands. The soldiers must soon have been followed by great numbers of settlers. Professor K. Cameron has argued that the Danes took over existing villages without changing their names, that the earliest Scandinavian place-names appear to be hybrids combining the Old English *ton* with a Danish personal name, as for example in Thurlstone, and that the Danes then settled on the less desirable sites that had not been colonised previously. A number of settlements in the lower Don valley have distinctive Danish names, including the ancient parish centres of Barnby Dun and Maltby, but they were more usually dependent territories such as Balby, Cadeby, Denaby, Hellaby, Scawsby, Armthorpe and Thorpe in Balne. It has been claimed that the sokemen recorded in Domesday Book are a particular feature of areas with strong Danish settlement, so it is interesting that over three-quarters of the West Riding sokemen were to be found in the south-east of the county, with just over half of them attached to the large fee of Conisbrough. In the western parts of South Yorkshire the proportion of Scandinavian names is much lower, though western hamlets such as Gunthwaite, Butterthwaite or Onesacre represent small clearings made by later Norwegian settlers, and the townships of Brightside and Ecclesall within the parish of Sheffield and of Brampton in the parish of Wath were long referred to as bierlows in the Viking manner. The *thorpe* hamlets in the west are also Danish in origin.

The Danes and the Norwegians left their mark on the administrative framework of Yorkshire, for ridings and wapentakes are Viking in origin and it was not until the reorganisation of local government in 1974 that these institutions were finally abolished. The South Yorkshire region came under the wapentakes of Staincross, of Strafforth (later Strafforth and Tickhill) and of part of Osgoldcross, whose centre lay near Pontefract. At first these courts were held in the open air at some convenient site near the centre of their territory. Staincross wapentake presumably met at or near the present village of that name, on a site marked by a stone cross, and Strafforth ('the street-ford') wapentake assembled near where the ancient Ricknield Street crossed the rivers Don and Dearne. Long after they had lost their judicial functions the wapentakes remained the units for collecting taxes and for raising the militia; their names were retained by educational and other local authorities until recently.

4 Ancient administrative units

Morthen   One of the units of Viking administration was already obsolete by the time of the Norman conquest. This was the district assembly known as the *thing*, a word that is incorporated in the name of the Tynwald, the upper house of the parliament of the Isle of Man, and in place-names such as Morthen, 'the moorland district with a common assembly.' The meetings of the Althing or General Assembly of tenth-century Iceland that are described so vividly in *Njal's Saga* give some idea of the proceedings of these open-air courts. The Althing was held for two weeks every June at Thingvellir ('Assembly Plains'), where accommodation was provided in semi-permanent booths; it was the main judicial, legislative and social event of the year. The Yorkshire assembly was divided into three regions known as trithings or ridings, and these in turn were divided into district assemblies, such as the one that was attended by local chieftains at Morthen. The actual meeting-place was probably in a hill-meadow to the left of the lane that follows the ridge from Upper Whiston to Morthen village, adjacent to the north-south trackway that crosses this lane at right angles. In 1345 a grant of 35¾ acres of land 'in the fields of Whitstan and Morthyng' included 'one plot of meadow called Tourneberg, in Whitstan and Morthyng field, on the east of the way leading from Roderham to Wirkesop.' The English Place-Name Society give the meaning of Tourneberg as 'the hill where the tourn or court was held,' and the exact identification of this site is made possible by a Fairbank survey of 1817 (in Sheffield Central Library) which records a meadow of four acres known as Turn Ing, just to the east of Upper Whiston and alongside the ancient track from Rotherham to Worksop. The site is a prominent one, conveniently near Ricknield Street and the north-south route through Rotherham along the present A618, and by the Roman road from Lincoln to Chester which passed immediately south of it. Now two stark rows of pylons and a motorway interchange act as signposts to this immemorial meeting-place.

Morthen had no administrative significance in the post-conquest period and it is impossible to fix its boundaries precisely, though it seems to have stretched from the county boundary on the eastern and southern sides of the parish of Laughton across to the River Rother or thereabouts. On several occasions Aston, Brampton, Dinnington and Laughton were described in medieval records as being 'in Morthing' or, in the Norman phrase, 'en le Morthen,' and to this day Brampton en le Morthen is so called to distinguish it from Brampton Bierlow. Morthen's description as a moorland district implies that it was centred upon the Coal-Measure sandstones, even though some of the places mentioned above stand on the Magnesian Limestone. The present Morthen place-names not only give a delightful sound to our villages; they are intriguing relics of a primitive Scandinavian organisation of about a thousand years ago.

Balne During the thirteenth and fourteenth centures several places bounded by the lower reaches of the Aire and the Don were described as being 'in Balne.' No sensible explanation has yet been offered for this ancient name and its antiquity can only be guessed at. There are, however, several parallels with Morthen. A township in the parish of Snaith is known simply as Balne, and Thorpe in Balne still retains the full name. Other places described at various times as having been 'in Balne' include Carlton, Fishlake, Heck, Moss, Moseley, Pollington, Stubbs and Sykehouse, and field names including the Balne element have been recorded in Campsall, Carcroft and Snaith. Eight of these places lie within South Yorkshire and the other five lie just to the north. Carlton was a detached portion of the parish of Snaith in Barkston Ash wapentake, but each of the others lay in the original wapentake of Osgoldcross before its southern parts were transferred to Strafforth and Tickhill in the early medieval period. By then Balne had lost any significance it may once have had.

Hallamshire Another ancient unit of administration was that of Hallamshire. The name is still used in the Sheffield region, but the exact nature of this 'shire' has long been forgotten and its precise boundaries have been a matter of dispute. In 1642 the bailiff of Sheffield thought that Hallamshire comprised the 72,000 or so acres of the parishes of Sheffield and Ecclesfield and the chapelry of Bradfield, and this in fact does seem to have been the full extent of the original lordship. The medieval lords of Sheffield added to their estates by acquiring neighbouring manors such as

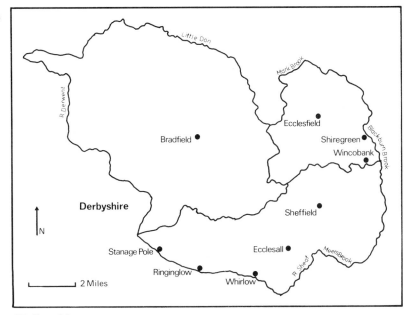

Hallamshire.

Handsworth, but these properties formed no part of the pre-conquest 'shire.' In 1268 Sheffield, Ecclesfield and Bradfield only were described as being within 'the metes of Halumshire.' It is worth looking at this lordship in some detail, for its history sheds much light on pre-conquest administrative arrangements.

In the absence of any documentary evidence before Domesday Book the essence of Hallamshire can be ascertained only by comparisons with such other northern 'shires' as Blackburnshire, Howdenshire, Richmondshire, Riponshire and Sowerbyshire. They and other lordships each lay within the Anglo-Saxon kingdom of Northumbria, whose southern boundary coincided with that of Hallamshire. This border followed the course of the River Sheaf, whose name means 'the boundary river,' and of the Meers Brook, 'the brook of the boundary.' It was an ancient and important frontier that separated Yorkshire from Derbyshire, the diocese of York from that of Lichfield, and Northumbria from Mercia. Thus, in 830, when the Northumbrians submitted to Egbert of Wessex in order to forestall an invasion, the ceremony was performed, symbolically, immediately across their boundary at Dore. The *Anglo-Saxon Chronicle* records further that in 942 Edmund, the son of Edward the Elder, conquered the Danes of Mercia 'as far as where Dore divides.'

The western boundary of Hallamshire was indicated by such prominent landmarks as Whirlow ('the boundary mound'), Stanage Pole, and 'a great heape of stones called Ringinglawe.' The south-western corner of the shire was contained within the township of Ecclesall, whose name was formed from *eccles*, a British church, and *halh*, one of whose meanings, appropriately, was 'land in an angle of a parish or county.' The northern and eastern boundaries followed the courses of the Little Don, the Don, the Mark Brook('the boundary brook') and the Blackburn Brook, as far as Shiregreen ('the common pasture or green on the shire bound'). The lordship was, thus, ten miles long and eight miles broad, forming a compact territory that was tucked away in the south-west corner of the county, the diocese, and the kingdom.

After studying the institutions of both Anglo-Saxon Northumbria and medieval Wales, J.E.A. Jolliffe concluded that, 'Northumbria shows so many parallels to Celtic custom that one is forced to suppose a historical continuity.' Hallamshire was probably already a recognisable unit during the period when the north of England was controlled by the Brigantes. This federation of Celtic tribes included the kingdom of Elmet, which lay east of the Pennines, south of the Wharfe, and west of the Humberhead levels. Its southern frontier is more difficult to fix. A 1281 reference to 'Alta Methelton in Elmete' can be identified only with High Melton, so the frontier must have been at least as far south as the Don, and possibly extended to what was later the county boundary. This view is reinforced by the evidence of the eighth-century *Tribal Hidage*, which refers to the most northerly tribes of the Mercians as the people of the Peak, of Elmet, and of Hatfield. As these tribes (two of which eventually returned to Northumbrian rule) shared common boundaries, the border between Elmet and the Peak must have been drawn somewhere in the Sheffield region.

Professor Glanville Jones has shown that a Celtic 'federal estate' had three points of focus; the administrative centre, the ecclesiastical centre, and the retreat in times of crisis. The retreat of the people of Hallamshire was the hill-fort at Wincobank, which protected the Don crossing, and which had once caused the Romans to delay their northern advance and to build their own fort on the opposite side of the river at Templeborough. The ecclesiastical centre is undoubtedly to be identified with Ecclesfield, whose name is derived from *eccles*, the Celtic word for a church. There may even have been a pre-Christian cult centre here, for a Celtic stone head of the type used in pagan ceremonies has been discovered in the lower end of the village. Ecclesfield's vast parish covered nearly 50,000 acres and included the huge chapelry of Bradfield. Not for nothing was the church known in 1620 as 'The Minster of the Moors.' Its parish had once been even larger, for it had originally served the whole of Hallamshire. As late as 1188 the monks of the Norman abbey of St Wandrille claimed that Sheffield was a chapelry dependent upon their church at Ecclesfield; and though Sheffield eventually became an independent parish, its former inferior status was acknowledged in 1291 and 1376. The monks also maintained that Whiston, which lay beyond Hallamshire to the south of Rotherham, was one of their chapelries. Furthermore, Aldwark Hall, to the north of Rotherham, remained a detached portion of the parish of Ecclesfield until the reign of Queen Victoria. (Seven miles away from Ecclesfield was another Celtic church within Hallamshire, at Ecclesall, but there is plenty of evidence from other parts of the country for such small, dependent churches, and independent parochial status was not achieved there until the nineteenth century.)

The third focal point of Hallamshire was the administrative centre, where, at the time of the Domesday Survey, Earl Waltheof had an aula, or hall. The meaning of the name Hallam is ambiguous, and the possible explanations do not help with the identification of the site. The absence of any earthwork, settlement, or convincing documentary evidence argues against the claims put forward for Hallam Head, and the best defensive site was undoubtedly at the confluence of the Sheaf and the Don at Sheffield, where the Normans erected their castle. Excavations under the Castle Market have revealed the presence of an Anglo-Saxon timber building of at least three bays, supported on crucks. It was almost certainly the aula of Waltheof. It was defended by steep slopes rising from the rivers and by a ditch to the east and the south. Fragments of eleventh-century pottery have been found at the bottom of this ditch. Topographical considerations enhance the claims of this site. In the *Quo Warranto* enquiries of the late thirteenth century, Thomas de Furnival, the lord of Sheffield, claimed among other things that his ancestors had enjoyed the privilege of a market and the right to hunt on their estates from the time of the conquest. This means that both the market and the park were in existence long before William de Lovetot erected his castle about the year 1100. Their relationship with the castle site is, therefore, of significance. The park lay directly across the River Sheaf from the castle, stretching from the Hallamshire boundary in the south to the Roman road from Lincoln to Chester in the north. It covered 2,461 acres and was the largest in South Yorkshire. The market occupied a large, rectangular site that lay across the Roman road immediately to the south of the castle. It is, of course, possible that de Lovetot created a new park and laid out a new market place upon building his castle, but a more likely explanation of these sites is that they are ancient ones that were associated with the aula of Waltheof. Sheffield, Ecclesfield and Wincobank seem to have been the three original centres of Hallamshire, and the experience of this 'shire' suggests the truth of the idea that, although administrative arrangements were in a constant state of flux, the basic framework often remained intact from Celtic times until well after the Norman conquest.

Conisbrough The most important administrative unit in Anglo-Scandinavian South Yorkshire was that based upon Conisbrough. Here overlooking the Don was a major military and ecclesiastical centre whose name means 'the king's stronghold'. At the time of the Norman conquest it was owned by King Harold, but as it was mentioned in the will of Wulfric Spott, a wealthy Mercian nobleman, in 1002-4, Conisbrough must be named after some earlier monarch. Unfortunately, nearly all its early history is based upon legend, and we can dismiss any stories of a connection with Hengest and Ambrosius as being the romantic invention of the medieval chronicler, Geoffrey of Monmouth. There is possibly some truth in the thirteenth-century account of Peter Langtoft that, four hundred years earlier, King Egbert was received here, at 'Burgh-Konan', but there is no supporting evidence in the *Anglo-Saxon Chronicle* or any other source. Recently, part of the earthworks of the Anglo-Saxon burh have been found within the Norman castle, and we may have more to learn from excavations on this site. In 1086 the fee, or lordship of Conisbrough included lands in 28 widely-scattered townships, most of which lay south of the Don, at Anston, Aston, Aughton, Barnburgh, Bilham, Braithwell, Bramley, Bramwith, Clifton, Cusworth, Dalton, Dinnington, Edenthorpe (formerly Stiresthorpe), Fishlake, Greasbrough, Hatfield, Harthill, Hoyland, Kirk Sandall, Long Sandall, Ravenfield, Stainforth, Thorne, Tudworth, Wales, Whiston and Wilsic. The soke of Doncaster, the honour of Tickhill and the Viking unit of 'Morthing' may well have been carved from the original fee, for Conisbrough's territory lay around and beyond them; indeed, Wulfric Spott's lands also included the adjoining Derbyshire manors of Barlborough, Beighton, Clowne, Duckmanton, Eckington, Mosbrough and Whitwell.

5   The earliest churches

Conisbrough was also an important minster or early ecclesiastical centre. We do not know when Christianity came to South Yorkshire but it was long before Augustine arrived at Canterbury in 597 or Paulinus baptised King Edwin of Northumbria at York 30 years later. Christianity had reached Roman Britain by the second or third century and had spread to the north by 314 when the bishop of York was one of three British clergymen at the Council of Arles. The documentary evidence for early Christian centres in South Yorkshire is lacking, but inferences about the most likely sites can nevertheless be drawn from place-names, the surviving architecture, and medieval relationships between mother and daughter churches. Thus, we have already seen that Ecclesfield was the minster or mother church for most of South-West Yorkshire, and that the name is derived from the Celtic word for a church. It may reasonably be deduced that the churches at both Ecclesfield and Ecclesall were still standing after the fall of the independent British kingdom of Elmet in the early seventh century and upon the arrival of the Anglo-Saxons, whom Paulinus was attempting to convert.

The earliest churches were probably of timber; just across the northern boundary of South Yorkshire the name of the tiny settlement of Felkirk means 'the church built of planks'. Soon, however, the Anglo-Saxons were erecting robust structures in local stone. The nave of St Peter's church at Conisbrough is undoubtedly ancient, and Mr Gerald Davies has argued persuasively that it bears a close resemblance to the eighth-century church further north at Ledsham, and thus to Benedict Biscop's church at Monkwearmouth. It is certainly at least a thousand years old. The nave is tall and narrow, with relatively thin walls and massive quoins laid in side-alternate fashion in the Northumbrian style. Furthermore, a blocked Anglo-Saxon window is apparent in the wall above the northern arcade. Two other blocked windows in the same wall, another above the south arcade, and a fourth one high above the chancel arch are Romanesque in style, but it is difficult to tell whether they are Anglo-Saxon or Norman. A sturdy tower was added early in the Norman period, then later in the twelfth century arches were knocked through the nave walls and aisles built to flank both the nave and the tower. The church was refashioned in the late Middle Ages so that there is now little external sign of its antiquity.

10

The Anglo-Saxon church of St Peter's, Conisbrough, was enlarged by the Normans. The large stones to the left formed the outer corner of the original building. Above the Norman arches is a small, blocked Anglo-Saxon window. St Peter's was the mother church for much of South Yorkshire.

Inside, however, it is obvious that this venerable building is the oldest standing structure in South Yorkshire.

The neighbouring parishes of Edlington and Warmsworth share Conisbrough's dedication to St Peter, and beyond lay a widely-scattered number of daughter churches. During the last decade of the eleventh century, William, second Earl of Warenne, granted Conisbrough and its dependent churches to the Cluniac priory that his father had founded upon his Sussex estate at Lewes. These churches each lay within the fee centred upon Conisbrough castle, at Braithwell, Dinnington, Fishlake, Harthill, Hatfield (with its chapel at Thorne), and Kirk Sandall (with its chapel at Armthorpe). At least three of these churches were pre-Norman foundations for they were recorded in Domesday Book and the western wall of the nave at Kirk Sandall appears to be earlier than the Norman south aisle. Early churches were normally associated with the secular estates of their founders, and if St Peter's is indeed an eighth century building, the fee of Conisbrough must have been an ancient lordship which covered that part of Northumbria that lay south of the Don and east of Hallamshire. It occupied a strategic position on the southern border of the kingdom and controlled the important crossing of the River Don at Strafford Sands.

Several medieval churches in the West Riding owed allegiance to Dewsbury, where one of a remarkable number of ninth-century sculptured stones was inscribed with the name of Paulinus. The Anglo-Saxon crosses found in Staincross wapentake at Cawthorne, High Hoyland and Penistone are similar in style to those further north in three of

11

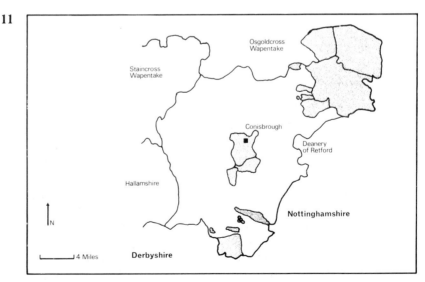

Conisbrough and its dependent parishes in the late eleventh century.

Dewsbury's daughter churches at Kirkburton, Kirkheaton and Thornhill. Most, if not all, of Staincross wapentake once lay within the parish of Silkstone, which included Barnsley, Cawthorne, Dodworth, Hoylandswaine, Stainborough and Thurgoland, and detached portions at Cumberworth and West Bretton. The area between the central and detached parts was served by the churches at Darton, High Hoyland and Penistone, whose administrative boundaries fit neatly into the overall shape of Silkstone parish. They may have been carved from the original unit in Anglo-Scandinavian or early-Norman times. However, there is some dispute as to whether the original church lay at Silkstone or Cawthorne. Rebuilding may explain why Silkstone church contains no architecture earlier than about 1200, whereas Cawthorne has two Anglo-Saxon crosses, but it is interesting that Domesday Book recorded a church and priest at Cawthorne but not at Silkstone. Part of Silkstone was dependent manorially upon Cawthorne and it is reasonable to expect the church to have been near the manor house. Only later subserviency argues against Cawthorne's claims to have been the mother church of Staincross wapentake. It was not unknown for ecclesiastical arrangements to be reversed after the Norman conquest. In Leicestershire, for example, Huncote lost its superior status to its former chapelry of Narborough; in Shropshire, Aldon became a dependent chapelry of its former daughter settlement at Stokesay; and in South Yorkshire, Tickhill took over the old parish of Dadsley. However, none of these churches was an ancient minster, so the argument cannot be proved either way. Ecclesfield, Conisbrough and either Silkstone or Cawthorne seem to have been the three minster churches of South Yorkshire.

In 633 Edwin of Northumbria was killed in battle with heathens, but two years later Oswald was able to revive part of this Christian kingdom. For a time South Yorkshire came under the dominion of Mercia, and even when it reverted to Northumbria it lay right on the southern frontier. Probably because of its border position, Austerfield was chosen in 702 as the meeting place of the synod which debated Wilfrid's claims to the see of York. Upon his accession, Oswald had invited Celtic monks from Iona to found a monastery at Lindisfarne and to preach to his subjects. During the next generation it was these monks rather than Roman missionaries who spread the faith in the north. In South Yorkshire, however, the Celtic influence was much weaker. Finningley and Kirk Sandall are dedicated to St Oswald, and Fishlake is dedicated to St Cuthbert, the most famous of the Celtic monks (whose body was reputedly rested here on its way to burial) but many more local churches honour St Peter and other saints who were popular with the Romans. Wickersley is dedicated to St Alban, and the patron saint of both Cantley and Hickleton is St Wilfrid, the man most responsible for the final triumph of the Roman organisation in Northumbria.

Nothing in the architecture of the little limestone church at Cantley suggests that it is in any way unusual, but the position that was chosen for it presents one of those puzzles which can never be satisfactorily solved but which make the study of early history so fascinating a pastime. The church is recorded in Domesday Book, and medieval documents speak of it as a joint venture of Branton and Cantley. However, it was not built alongside the highway between these two villages, but by a minor lane beyond Cantley. Modern housing development has obscured the fact that the church is in a position that is inconvenient for both of these old settlements. It stands on a slight mound and, instead of facing more-or-less due east in the normal manner, it is orientated 40 degrees to the north. There must have been some very special reason for this choice of site. The church stood alongside the road from Bawtry to Danum and by the road that went through the second-century pottery kilns to the Don at Wheatley. Its dedication to Wilfrid hints at the Roman connection and suggests an early foundation. The mystery cannot be explained adequately, but it is possible that Cantley church was founded upon a site that had associations with earlier forms of worship. An assumption that the church replaced a Romano-British pagan temple or burial ground associated with the pottery kilns makes some sense of the strange orientation, the dedication, and the choice of site. Pope Gregory instructed his missionaries to Britain not to alienate the native population by the wholesale destruction of their religious buildings, but rather to convert heathen temples to Christian use by replacing idols with altars.

Seven miles further north the Roman road serves as the parish boundary of Adwick le Street. The place-name is said to mean 'Adda's dairy farm', but another possibility is that it is derived from *vicus*, a Roman village, for it lies only four miles north of Danum and a Roman or early-Saxon cemetery has been found within its bounds. The church of St Lawrence shares Cantley's curious orientation, some 40 degrees to the north-east, and the surrounding field boundaries point in the same direction. At the moment we can only ponder on this and note that in Germany the name of St Lawrence is commonly attached to churches of Roman origin. (Hatfield, South Yorkshire's only other example, was originally dedicated to St Mary).

Fifteen places in South Yorkshire had a church recorded in Domesday Book. The list is incomplete, for no church is mentioned at Laughton, despite the Anglo-Saxon work there. It is obvious from other parts of the country that the Domesday survey was not too concerned with ecclesiastical matters. On the other hand, the list does show that the Christian faith was widespread in the county and that churches had been established even in such small places as Aston, Barnby Dun, Todwick and Treeton. Anglo-Saxon crosses in various states of preservation survive as standing structures or have been incorporated in the masonry of churches at Barnburgh, Bradfield, Cawthorne, Conisbrough, Ecclesfield, High Hoyland, High Melton, Mexborough, Penistone, Sheffield, Sprotbrough and Thrybergh. Some may have been preaching crosses before churches were built, others may have been commemorative stones. The Normans seem to have had little regard for them and to have re-used them as building material. The finest fragment to survive is that of the tenth-century Sheffield cross, which is decorated with vine scrolls, bunches of grapes, and the carved figure of a man with a bow-and-arrow. It is kept in the British Museum, but a cast is on display in Sheffield City Museum.

12

The tenth-century Sheffield cross is possibly 'the great cross in the churchyard' which was pulled down in 1570. Now in the British Museum, it was found last century in a cutler's workshop with one side hollowed out as a hardening trough. A cast is on display in Sheffield City Museum. (From W.G. Collingwood, Northumbrian Crosses of the Pre-Norman Age, *1927, p75)*

Two other South Yorkshire churches are basically Anglo-Saxon in structure. At Bolton upon Dearne the nave is typically tall and narrow, with walls that are only three feet thick. The corner-stones are massive slabs laid in the long-and-short fashion that was common in eleventh-century Mercia, but rare in the north. A typical round-headed, splayed window survives in the south wall, and nearby is a blocked opening which may have led to a porticus, or side-chapel. Its jambs consist of through stones laid alternately upright and flat in the Northumbrian style. The Anglo-Saxon work is particularly evident on the outside of the south wall. The other church is the beautiful little building at Burghwallis, which has an astonishing amount of herringbone walling on its south side. This is usually held to be an early-Norman feature, but on the other hand, the relatively thin walls, the massive side-alternate quoins and the dimensions of both the nave and the chancel are Anglo-Saxon rather than Norman. The tower has no herring-boning and is obviously a little later in style. The church appears to have been built in two stages by native craftsmen either not long before or not long after the Norman conquest. The county's other ancient churches are rebuildings or new foundations of the Norman and early-medieval period. Not until the twelfth century was the division of the original minster territories into parishes completed.

Most of the present towns and villages of South Yorkshire had received their first settlers by the time that Domesday Book was compiled in 1086, and many hamlets, too, were already in existence. Colonies of pastoral farmers had established themselves on the fen islands in the east, and on the Pennines pioneer farmers at Ughill were growing crops and

13

The attractive small church of St Helen's, Burghwallis, has herringbone walls that are late Anglo-Saxon or early Norman. The tower was added a little later.

raising livestock just below the 1,000 foot contour. On the Coal-Measures many of the woods had been felled, and on the Magnesian Limestone some parishes had brought almost all their territory under cultivation. Over 1,600 acres were being tilled around Harthill and Kiveton, and roughly similar amounts were being cultivated at Braithwell, at Todwick and at Wadworth. Of course, a great amount of land still lay waste, but by 1086 many features of our present landscape were already recognisable.

6 Laughton en le Morthen

The pattern of settlement that had been established by the time of the Norman conquest can best be illustrated by examining one parish in detail The visitor who is attracted to the peaceful village of Laughton en le Morthen, set dramatically upon a hill amidst the corn fields and woods of its large parish, is rewarded immediately by the sight of one of the most splendid church spires in the county. The dedication to All Saints suggests a pre-conquest foundation, and this suggestion is confirmed by the design of the doorway which once led into the northern porticus, or side-chapel, of the Anglo-Saxon church. This doorway is 10ft 2in tall and 3ft 4in wide, and the surrounding wall is 2ft 8in to 2ft 10in thick, with quoins arranged in the 'long-and-short' method, as at Bolton. This part of the building is constructed of 'Rotherham red' sandstone from nearby quarries, and is in marked contrast to the limestone that was used in the later rebuilding.

14

Laughton en le Morthen church is an Anglo-Saxon foundation that was rebuilt in two phases, culminating in the magnificent tower and spire, a landmark for miles around

However, the base of the chancel is also formed of red sandstone, buttressed by thin Norman pilasters of Magnesian Limestone. It is difficult to say whether this is the original Anglo-Saxon chancel or whether the surviving masonry is re-used material from an earlier building. A triangular-headed piscina in the internal south wall lends support to the belief that this is original Anglo-Saxon work. The church is, therefore, of great interest, and the fascination of the village becomes compelling when it is seen that just beyond the western edge of the churchyard is the grassy earthwork of a motte-and-bailey castle, now subdued and superfluous, standing in silent testimony to a bygone, heroic age.

The fertility of the soils that overlie the Magnesian Limestone encouraged settlers from the earliest periods of which we have knowledge. By the time of the Norman conquest this arable belt was the most prosperous and the most densely settled of any part of the West Riding.

15

The north door of All Saints' church, Laughton en le Morthen, is Anglo-Saxon. The Normans preserved this stretch of wall when they rebuilt the church, but inserted a smaller door of their own.

The typical form of settlement in this region was the small parish with a nucleated village surrounded by its open fields, but Laughton parish was rather different, for it was by far the largest on the Magnesian Limestone.

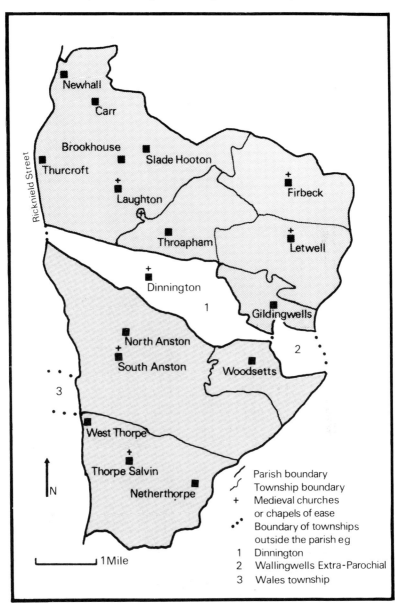

The parish of Laughton en le Morthen, detached portions of which are contained within the township of Wales. (Detached portions of Conisbrough parish are also contained within the township of Anston).

It was divided into chapelries by early Norman times, and from the reign of Henry I onwards it belonged to the Dean and Chapter of York and was not therefore included with the greater part of the parishes of South Yorkshire within the deanery of Doncaster.

The ancient parish of Laughton was bounded on the south and the east by the counties of Derbyshire and Nottinghamshire, on the north by the parish of Maltby, and on the west by Ricknield Street. Three 'thorpes,' or outlying settlements, were established from Danish times onwards in the south of the parish. West Thorpe lay on the prehistoric ridgeway and in earlier times was known as Ricknieldthorpe; Nether Thorpe is now marked by a moated site; and a Norman church was built at Thorpe Salvin, which was distinguished from the other thorpes by the name of its manorial lords. Several other settlements were established within the parish of Laughton before the Norman conquest. Each of them lay in the western part, near the street and away from the woods which covered so much of the eastern half of the parish. In the north-west, Newhall has an obvious meaning as a place-name; about 400 acres of land were cultivated here in 1066, and it never grew into a village. Hooton was originally just a farm on a spur of land, which acquired the prefix Slade from the valley below in order to distinguish it from the other Hootons, such as Hooton Pagnell and Hooton Roberts. Throapham is a much more difficult name, which may possibly refer to the settlement's dependent status; in Domesday Book (where it was spelt *Trapun*) it was described as a berewick, or outlying farmstead of Laughton. The curious position of its church, at the southern edge of Laughton village, will be discussed later. Further south, the manorial and parochial framework is less straight-forward, and the sequence of colonisation is not as apparent. In the first place, a small part of North Anston and a major share of Dinnington belonged to the fee of Conisbrough and were dependent ecclesiastically upon St Peter's, the minster church at the head of the fee, even though they were almost completely surrounded by townships that lay within the soke and parish of Laughton. On the other hand, detached portions of Laughton lay beyond Ricknield Street in the township of Wales, whose name means 'the territory of the Welshmen.' Here were a group of those Celtic survivors who lived in a separate settlement at the edge of the Anglo-Saxon and Danish estates. Most of the township of Wales was independent manorially and formed part of the neighbouring parish of Harthill, and it is no longer clear why portions of it were included with Laughton.

Apparently no farmers had settled in the eastern half of the parish by the time that Domesday Book was compiled. Firbeck and Letwell are unrecorded before the twelfth century, and Gildingwells and Woodsetts are not mentioned for another two hundred years. Most of the early references to these places in fact relate to natural features in the landscape and not to actual settlements. In the western half of the parish only

Brookhouse and Thurcroft were settled at a comparatively late date (being first recorded in 1297 and 1319, respectively), whereas in the east the clearing of the woods proceeded so slowly that a tract of land beyond Gildingwells and Woodsetts was cultivated not by the men of Laughton but by pioneers from Nottinghamshire. Even though this tract lay within Yorkshire, it remained part of the parish of Wallingwells throughout the medieval period and in 1974 was transferred to Nottinghamshire. Nevertheless, 54 carucates of land, that is something in the order of 6,000 acres, had already been cleared for cultivation in the lordship or 'soke' of Laughton by the time of the Norman conquest. Twelve carucates had been cleared around Laughton village, six carucates in Throapham, and a further thirty-six in outlying areas. Edwin, Earl of Mercia, was the last Anglo-Danish lord of the soke of Laughton, and here he had a hall or 'aula.' Domesday references to such aulas are rare indeed; the only other one in the whole of South Yorkshire was the hall of Waltheof in Hallamshire.

The earthworks of Laughton's motte-and-bailey castle stand immediately to the west of the church, on the edge of an easily-defended outlier of Magnesian Limestone. The motte is 30 feet high and 30 feet in diameter at the top and is surrounded by a deep ditch. The bailey covers about half an acre, and the whole structure is well preserved. The controversy as to whether or not such castles were occasionally erected in England before the Norman conquest has not yet been resolved. They were certainly a Norman invention, but by 1066 the leaders of English society had absorbed much of the Norman culture. That being so, the Domesday reference to Earl Edwin's aula makes Laughton's earthworks worthy of particular attention. The site needs to be excavated in order to determine whether the earthworks are those of the aula or whether Edwin's hall was destroyed and new defences erected in its place. After the Norman conquest the soke of Laughton was absorbed within the newly-created lordship or 'honour' of Tickhill, but it is interesting that in Domesday Book the possessions of Roger de Busli, the Norman lord, were headed not by Tickhill but by Laughton. The aula survived in name long after the conquest, for in 1088 de Busli's foundation charter for Blyth priory granted the monks (among other things) two parts of the tithes of the land of the aula. Laughton retained a special role within the honour of Tickhill as the seat of one of the honorial courts, and was referred to as a barony in the Hundred Rolls of 1276. It was still a relatively large place in 1379 when the poll tax returns named 238 people over the age of sixteen. This continued prosperity is reflected by the architecture of All Saints' church. The Normans rebuilt the Anglo-Saxon structure towards the end of the twelfth century, and about two hundred years later the building was refashioned in the style we see today. The magnificent spire, 'designed with considerable originality and ingenuity' (Pevsner), is one of the outstanding achievements of late-medieval Yorkshire.

The Middle Ages

7 Castles

In 1066 five of the mightiest Anglo-Scandinavian earls in the country owned land in South Yorkshire: Harold had Conisbrough, Tostig held Doncaster, Waltheof had Hallamshire, Morcar owned five small manors, and Edwin was lord of the soke of Laughton and of Hooton Pagnell. All except Waltheof lost their possessions after the battle of Hastings or after the 1069 rebellion of the northern earls, and Waltheof was beheaded for conspiracy in 1075.

The Normans imposed radical political and military changes in South Yorkshire by creating a lordship and two boroughs in the south-east of the county. The typical northern lordship (which was described variously as a barony, fee, honour, liberty, lordship or soke) was very different from the village-manor that was usual in much of central and southern England. In the north, a lordship contained very little demesne land, but had many dependent vills and sub-manors that were often several miles from the centre of administration at the castle. The Normans built three substantial castles in South Yorkshire; two of them upon ancient strongholds at Conisbrough and Sheffield, and a third upon a new site near the county boundary at Tickhill. Furthermore, the townships of Staincross wapentake and a few manors to the north of the lower reaches of the Don passed under the domination of the de Lacis at Pontefract Castle and were eventually absorbed within the Duchy of Lancaster.

Motte-and-baileys   The three large castles were the product of an age when Norman rule was no longer actively disputed. Their purpose was not merely to act as a refuge but to dominate an area. In earlier times, immediately after the conquest and during the civil wars of the reign of Stephen, the defences that were hastily constructed were motte-and-bailey earthworks surmounted with a timber stockade and, often, a wooden tower. Built by forced labour, these private forts of the Norman lords and their retinues were formidable strongholds. The *Anglo-Saxon Chronicle* says tersely of William, 'Castles he caused to be made, and poor men to be greatly oppressed', and of the reign of Stephen (1135-54), 'They filled the whole land with these castles. They sorely burdened the unhappy people of the country with forced labour on the castles. And when the castles were made they filled them with devils and wicked men.' Motte-

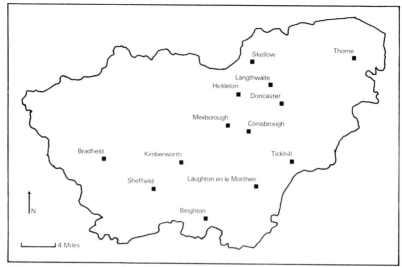

Motte and bailey castles.

and-baileys are rarely mentioned in this poorly-documented period, and some of their earthworks have been destroyed for ever. Nevertheless, at least thirteen sites are known in South Yorkshire, and a high proportion of them were constructed on or near the Magnesian Limestone belt, that area of early settlement in the central part of the county. Most were strategically placed so as to control the major roads and the important river crossings.

Mottes were artificial mounds of stone and earth, round or oval at the base and flattened at the top, so as to provide a vantage point, a final defence post, and sometimes a temporary residence. The baileys contained the outbuildings and were shaped to suit the lie of the land. The whole complex was surrounded by a ditch which was crossed by a removable wooden bridge. The best surviving examples are the earthworks at Laughton (which have been described earlier) and those at Bradfield within the lordship at Hallamshire. Castle Hill at Bradfield seems to be a natural feature rather than a fortified site, though it may have been used as a look-out point; there is no doubt, however, about the earthworks on nearby Bailey Hill, for here is one of the best preserved and most dramatic motte-and-baileys in Yorkshire. The substantial motte is 60 feet high and is protected by a steep ditch; an amateur excavation about 1720 revealed squared stones with the marks of a tool upon them. The eastern and southern sides of the ¾ acre bailey are enclosed by a curving rampart, which is 310 feet long and is still 30 feet high from the bottom of the surrounding ditch. The western edge is protected by a prodigiously steep cliff, and though the earthwork is now covered with trees, it still looks awesome in winter. The site was originally a wild one, but the castle soon attracted a church and a hamlet alongside it.

An interesting site which is best visited in winter when the grass is low is to be found at the deserted hamlet of Langthwaite, two miles north of Doncaster. Here was a small manor held by the Fossards, the Norman lords of the soke of Doncaster. Although the motte is now only sixteen feet high, the plan of the earthwork is well preserved, with a 40 feet wide ditch encircling the motte and the bean-shaped, ½ acre bailey. Marshy land presumably protected this low-lying site, and the north-western side was strengthened by a small annexe. A similar plan can be observed at Mexborough, overlooking the important crossing of the River Don at Strafford Sands on the opposite side of the highway to Conisbrough. In the Middle Ages one of the great courts of the honour of Tickhill was held here. The motte has been reduced in size and the site is now used as a public garden, but the ditches that surround the motte and the ½ acre bailey are 50 feet wide and quite well preserved.

The large motte known as Peel Hill can still be found to the north of the church at Thorne. An early-fifteenth century map of Inclesmoor marks a stone tower on this motte, and stone foundations are still partly visible. Peel Hill lay within the Conisbrough fee and in later times may possibly have been used as a hunting seat within Hatfield Chase. The motte is 22 feet high and 55 feet in diameter on top, but though its surrounding ditch is well preserved there is now no trace of any bailey. Further north, at Skellow, the site known as Cromwell's Batteries is much older than the name suggests. A motte is preserved in the grounds of Skellow Hall and the bailey can be partly traced in a field to the north, where it is cut across by Hampole Balk road. A possible site a mile or so to the west, on the other side of the Roman road, at Hampole is known as Castle Hill, but it has been destroyed by deep ploughing.

Yet another motte is now surrounded by a housing estate south of the

18

The motte-and-bailey earthworks at Langthwaite are well preserved and waterlogged and therefore a prime choice for future excavation. Probably erected by the Fossards, the Norman lords of Doncaster, this castle was later replaced by the nearby Radcliffe moat.

Wortley road at Kimberworth, but the bailey has gone. Nor are there many surface indications at a site at Beighton, suggested by an early thirteenth century reference to 'the tower of the former castle.' The earthworks at Castle Hill, Hickleton, have been destroyed by quarrying, but the tradition preserved by the name is an accurate one, for a sketch by the antiquary, Roger Dodsworth, shows that in the seventeenth century the outlines of a motte-and-bailey were still clear. There may have been other sites for which we have neither archaeological nor documentary evidence. However, the 'Castle Mound,' which is hidden by trees on a small plateau alongside the A1 motorway, is in fact the 'temple hill' which was constructed as a feature of Cusworth Park in 1762-3, complete with 'a fine slope and ha-ha', and castle place-names at Langsett and Rough Birchworth refer not to motte-and-baileys, but to earlier fortifications dating from the Iron Age.

Keep-and-baileys From the second half of the twelfth century onwards the most important castles were given stone keeps and stone walls in place of the old timber defences. The great majority of these keep-and-bailey castles were adaptations of existing strongholds; the motte-and-baileys which were not adapted in this way gradually fell into disuse. The most spectacular military monument in South Yorkshire, and one of the finest in the land, is Conisbrough castle, which is set in a magnificent position overlooking the narrow valley that the River Don has cut through the Magnesian Limestone. Conisbrough was held from 1163 to 1202 by a half-brother of Henry II, Hameline Plantagenet, who had married the daughter of the last of the Norman Warennes. The impressive 90 feet high keep was a larger and better version of a similar keep that he had erected upon his estate in Normandy. He seems to have built at Conisbrough during the 1170s, for the constable of the castle witnessed a document that

19

Conisbrough Castle, the outstanding medieval monument in South Yorkshire, was built by Hameline Plantagenet in the 1170s. The keep is one of the finest in the country and was one of the first to be built on a cylindrical plan. The outer walls had begun to collapse by the late fifteenth century.

can be dated to 1174-8, and the chapel of the keep is mentioned during the 1180s. The pilaster buttresses of the curtain wall and the mouldings in the chapel are typical features of this period. The keep is built in local stone, faced with ashlar, and is one of the earliest examples of the cylindrical plan, first introduced into this country at Orford in Suffolk. Supported by six great buttresses and a spreading plinth, the keep is 52 feet in diameter at first floor level and the walls are fifteen feet thick. For security reasons, the basement room has no windows and the main entrance is twenty feet above ground; furthermore, there was an adequate water supply from the well in the centre of the floor.

A staircase in the walls led to the hall, or main living room, on the next floor. The large fireplace in the north-west buttress is particularly interesting as the method of joining the stones was a middle-eastern practice that may well have been introduced into Europe by the victorious crusaders. The hall also has a small window, a sink, and a garderobe or latrine passage. The solar room above was reached by a staircase on the opposite side to the lower one. It has a similar fireplace, window, sink and latrine, and in the south-east buttress is a small vaulted chapel with some fine late-Norman carvings. The top floor originally contained a small guard room, two cisterns, an oven and what seems to have been a dovecote; it must also have had a conical roof, but that has long since gone.

The foundations of other buildings have been revealed by excavations within the inner bailey. Much of the curtain wall and the semi-circular towers survive, though by the fifteenth century the rubble interior had started to collapse. The walls are about 35 feet high and appear to be contemporary with the keep, but it was thought that the towers were added about twenty years later. The castle was defended by steep banks on all sides except the west, where there is a curved outer bailey beyond the deep moat. To complete the defences, a gatehouse was built with a barbican (ie a passage between high walls) that would have forced any attackers to turn 45 degrees to the right and then 90 degrees to the left to face the gateway. But, as far as is known, no battle ever took place here. The castle fell into disuse in the late fifteenth century and was already beyond repair by the reign of Henry VIII. It owes its preservation to the fact that it was never garrisoned during the Civil War and was not, therefore, demolished, as were Sheffield and Tickhill castles, once Charles I had been defeated.

After the Norman conquest, Harold's possessions had been given to William de Warenne, a distinguished commander at the battle of Hastings. He acquired large estates in many parts of England and built castles at Lewes, Reigate, Sandall and Castle Acre. An enormous hunting park that was probably pre-conquest in origin was associated with the castle at Conisbrough, and the Norman lords seem to have been interested in the place only for military and hunting purposes. No attempt seems to have been made to develop Conisbrough as a commercial centre, for there is no evidence of any markets or fairs being held there. This is surprising in view of the past importance of the place and of its accessibility along ancient routes. Conisbrough would have fared better under lords who were less distinguished but always resident. As it was, it lost its ecclesiastical supremacy when the Normans created the deanery of Doncaster (which covered most of the present county of South Yorkshire) and it declined in status once the great age of castles was over. Of the forty-seven married couples and fifty-four single persons who paid the poll tax in 1379, only three people were assessed at more than the basic rate of fourpence. The merchants or tradesmen rich enough to be taxed on a higher scale were missing.

The Normans built another major castle at Tickhill, six miles south-east of Conisbrough, near the Nottinghamshire boundary. The Domesday survey of 1086 shows that Roger de Busli had been granted extensive estates in South Yorkshire, including Waltheof's former liberty of Hallamshire and Earl Edwin's soke of Laughton. The new honour or lordship of Tickhill was to be a major political force whose influence was felt for centuries. It had numerous dependent manors in the south of the county (some of which were intermingled with the Conisbrough fee) and it also included a group that lay further north in an unbroken line from Wentworth in the west to Barnby Dun in the east. Other dependent manors were to be found scattered in Nottinghamshire, Derbyshire, Lincolnshire and Leicestershire; in fact only a third of the honour lay within Yorkshire.

Of all the old towns in South Yorkshire Tickhill has the most appeal for its connections with a more important past are immediately recognisable and its character has not been altered by industrialisation. Domesday Book refers not to Tickhill but to Dadsley, an Anglo-Saxon settlement whose name means 'Daeddi's clearing'. The location of this settlement is a matter of dispute, and the problem can be solved only by an extensive programme of excavations. One theory maintains that as Dadsley was described in Domesday Book as a borough the site should be marked by a pattern of burgage tenements, which must lie under part of modern Tickhill. Against this it can be argued that the only other West Riding borough recorded in Domesday Book was known by the old name of Tanshelf, despite the fact that the burgesses occupied a new site not far away at Pontefract. The second theory says that Tickhill was a new settlement laid out shortly after the Norman conquest and that Dadsley was a village or hamlet half a mile or so to the north, near Dadsley Lane and Dadsley Well, where a number of country lanes converge. Significantly, the road out of Tickhill bends sharply upon leaving Northgate, as if to return to the old alignment. The pattern of the ancient open fields supports this theory, with Eastfield lying directly east of Dadsley Well Farm. Despite all this no signs of an Anglo-Saxon settlement have so far been found either on the ground or from the air. If such a village existed it possibly lay near Dadsley Well rather than around the knoll where the foundations of All Hallows church can be traced. Perhaps the church's remote position was chosen as a central point for a number of scattered settlements such as Stancil, Wellingley, Wilsic and Woolthwaite, but whatever the reason All Hallows was doubtless the parish church before St Mary's was built at the edge of the new town of Tickhill.

The natural feature that formed the bottom part of the castle motte is the only topographical feature that can account for Tickhill's name: the hill of some unknown Tica. The original castle was a motte-and-bailey of considerable size, for the motte is 75 feet high and 80 feet in diameter at the top and the bailey covers two acres. Beyond the massive rampart of the bailey is a deep ditch, which is 30 feet wide and still filled with water in its southern and western parts. Roger de Busli's lands passed to Robert de Belleme, earl of Shrewsbury, who backed the wrong successor to the throne and in 1102 fortified his castles of Arundel, Tickhill, Bridgnorth and Shrewsbury against King Henry I. All the castles were reduced within a month and Robert was banished. Henry I was received at Tickhill and from that time the honour belonged to the Crown. The Pipe Rolls for 1129-30 show that nearly £30 was spent on alterations that were designed to strengthen the castle; the money probably went towards the gatehouse and the curtain wall that was erected on top of the rampart. Between 1178 and 1182 Henry II spent a further £138 on a keep and a stone bridge; and Queen Eleanor founded a chapel dedicated to St Nicholas. During

20

An aerial view of Tickhill castle, which was dismantled in 1648 after the defeat of the royalist forces in the Civil War. The tremendous motte which supported the keep is still evident, but the deep moat is obscured by trees. Fishponds and a hunting park lay immediately beyond the castle. (Cambridge University Collection, Copyright Reserved)

The Norman gatehouse of Tickhill castle was erected in 1129-30 by King Henry I. The walls in the foreground were built in the late Middle Ages to support a drawbridge.

Richard I's absence on the crusades fresh trouble erupted, for in 1191 John seized the castles of Tickhill and Nottingham. By 1194 the rebellion was largely suppressed, but when John came to the throne in 1199 he acquired Tickhill and during his reign spent well over £300 on strengthening the castle defences. For over a century Tickhill was peaceful, but in the autumn of 1321 Thomas, Earl of Lancaster, tried to summon a parliament to meet at Doncaster, and in the ensuing civil war Tickhill castle was besieged for three weeks in February 1322. Three centuries after Lancaster's failure Tickhill was the scene of action during the Civil War of the reign of Charles I. In 1648, after the defeat of the royalist forces, the keep was dismantled but its ground plan has been revealed by excavation. It stood on the line of the curtain wall, as at Conisbrough, and consisted of an eleven-sided tower placed upon a circular plinth and supported at the angles by typical Norman pilaster buttresses.

8 Towns

Tickhill Tickhill acquired markets and fairs long before the system of issuing royal licences was begun late in the twelfth century; they probably date from the foundation of the town. The main streets or 'gates' converge upon the market square, which lies some distance away from the castle. The original castle green or outer bailey may have extended almost as far as the square to a curving ditch, ten feet deep and fifteen feet wide, which has recently been discovered by excavation. This ditch was an early feature, for it was later filled in to allow the extension of a narrow burgage plot back towards St Mary's Road. The area around the market place is known as Sunderland, which means 'land set apart for a special purpose,' quite possibly land which was 'sundered' by this ditch. A parliamentary survey of 1649 speaks of 'The Burgar or gate rent payable within a certain streete . . . called Sunderland,' and 'The tolls of waggons, cartes and all other carriages and drifts passing in or through the way or streete called Sunderland.' The old administrative division lingered long in official memory, and as late as the hearth tax returns of 1672 Sunderland was still recorded separately from the rest of Tickhill.

The town grew rapidly and the pattern of burgage plots is preserved by long gardens and rows of outbuildings, especially between the main street and the back lane known as St Mary's Road. The plots on the valuable sites near the market place are much narrower than those further out, and the dog-leg shape of Castlegate suggests that the town grew from the market place towards the castle. Recent excavations have failed to find any early buildings in the large green area outside the castle moat. During the early thirteenth century St Mary's church was erected just beyond this green at the edge of the growing town. Its dedication was fashionable at this time and became popular much later than that of All Hallows, whose church it replaced as the parish centre. The curving boundaries of some of the burgage plots and the narrow passage-ways add support to the theory that Tickhill was laid out on a virgin site, for it is possible that these curves follow the ridge-and-furrow patterns of open-field agriculture.

During the fourteenth and fifteenth centuries St Mary's church was enlarged and re-styled until it was one of the most splendid in the region. Tickhill also boasted an Augustinian friary, which was founded at the west end of the town about 1260. About eighteen friars lived here in 1300 and 35 years later the number had risen to twenty-four. A thirteenth-century lancet window and some later masonry from this friary are incorporated in the house that now occupies the site, and a thirteenth-century archway adorns the garden. The numbers had shrunk to eight by the time the friary was dissolved in 1538. The religious orders also served a Maison Dieu (founded about 1199), whose memory is preserved by the modern cottages south of the church, and St Leonard's hospital, which was established

St Leonard's hospital, Tickhill, is a timber-framed building dating from 1470. The upper floor was completely rebuilt in mock-medieval style in 1851. It has recently been carefully restored.

about 1225 and became dependent upon Humberston abbey. As this hospital was principally for lepers in its early years it may have been the one which accounts for the name Spital Hill at the far end of Eastgate, well away from the town. The treatment of lepers must have ceased by 1470 when a timber structure of ten bays (much restored in 1851) was erected at the edge of the market place. In addition to these public buildings, there were four chantry chapels attached to the church, a private chapel in the castle, and an ancient school. As the administrative centre of a large honour Tickhill was one of the most important places in early medieval Yorkshire. In 1334 it was the second wealthiest town in South Yorkshire, and by 1379 it contained 176 married couples and 109 single persons over the age of sixteen, including the great variety of craftsmen that were necessary in a market town. Several merchants are named in various taxation lists, and Tickhill became one of the most successful of the many new towns of early medieval England.

Doncaster   A borough was created by the Normans at Doncaster after the soke had been granted to Nigel Fossard upon the banishment of the Conqueror's half brother, Robert, Count of Mortain. The Domesday Book reference to Doncaster is baffling, for all the manors that formed the soke were apparently dependent upon Hexthorpe, which is now a Doncaster suburb and whose place-name is that of a minor Danish settlement, or upon Wheatley. Yet it is known that the Roman fort of Danum, upon and around which modern Doncaster is built, was superseded by an Anglo-Saxon burh before the building of the Norman castle, for excavations have unearthed a fourteen-feet deep ditch to the east of Danum and double ditches to the south. Furthermore, Doncaster appears as a place-name in Wulfric Spott's will in 1002-4. An interesting parallel is found at Chesterfield, another Roman fort whose site has been re-occupied and whose fortifications explain the present name of the town; here the Domesday manor was administered from Newbold, a new settlement that now forms a suburb of the town. How far Roman sites were occupied during the Dark Ages before the Norman conquest is a question that has not yet been answered by urban archaeologists, though currently it is receiving much attention. It is unlikely that Doncaster was neglected for long, for here was a strategic site where the highway that was to become known as the Great North Road crossed the River Don at its highest navigable point for coastal traffic. Although there were no burgesses in Doncaster when Domesday Book was compiled, a borough had been established before Richard I's charter of 1194 formalised previous traditions and old usages. Doncaster was fully incorporated in 1467 with a ruling body consisting of a mayor, twelve aldermen and twenty-four common councilmen, who were described later as being 'of the more excellent reputable and discreet inhabitants.' From the late fifteenth century onwards the corporation also acted as manorial lords over the ancient soke, which included Balby, Hexthorpe, Long Sandall, Loversall, Potteric Carr, Rossington and Wheatley, and small detached portions further north at Langthwaite and Tilts.

Nothing can now be seen of the castle, but the former motte has been located under the eastern end of St George's church and it has been shown that the surrounding ditch was sixteen feet deep and 30 feet wide. The Norman borough was laid out near the castle and alongside the Roman road, and its plan is preserved in the present street alignments. Burgage plots have been traced in French Gate, High Street, St Sepulchre Gate and in the streets leading to the market place, notably Baxter Gate (where the bakers were congregated) and Scot Lane (where market tolls were paid). By 1215, and possibly long before, the entire town was enclosed with an earthen rampart and ditch, which was filled with water from the Cheswold, the original course of the Don, now concealed from view. Doncaster never had walls like York or Chester, but the four entrances at St Mary's Bridge, St Sepulchre Gate, Hall Gate and Sun Bar were substantial stone gates; both they and the ditch (which was filled up in 1734) have had a fundamental effect on the topography of the town right up to the present day.

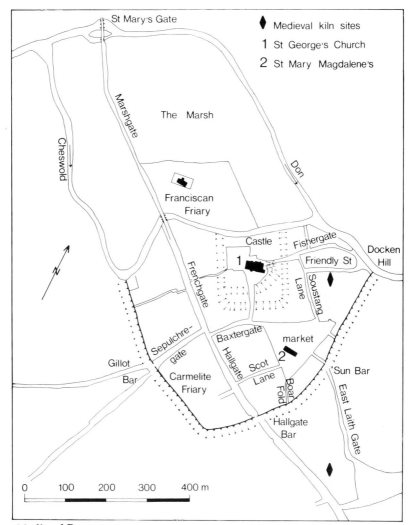

Medieval Doncaster.

Doncaster was the most prosperous medieval town in South Yorkshire. In 1334 its inhabitants contributed £17 in taxes, compared with £12 10s 0d from Tickhill and £7 3s 4d from Sheffield. Until the coming of the railways in the nineteenth century Doncaster owed its wealth chiefly to its weekly markets and annual fairs, both of which became nationally famous. A huge market place was laid out in the south-east corner of the medieval town, just inside the ditch and ramparts and alongside the wharf. It had long been in existence by 1199 when a royal charter extended the fair from two to three days, and like many other early market places it appears to have been an extension of the churchyard. Medieval Doncaster had two churches built in the Norman style, namely St George's, which lay within the bounds of the castle, and St Mary Magdalene's, which stood in the market place. Folk memory and scattered documentary references spoke of the former existence of St Mary Magdalene's, but when the Elizabethan town hall and grammar school were demolished in 1846, no-one was prepared for the dramatic exposure of a Norman nave of six bays, with part of a clerestory and a chancel arch. It is now generally accepted that St Mary Magdalene's was the original parish church. St George's dedication was fashionable at a relatively late period, and the site did not become available until the castle was demolished. The medieval churchyard coincided exactly with the area of the former bailey. Once the castle had fallen into disuse and the pressure upon the available space for marketing had increased, the old church was abandoned in favour of the new. St Mary Magdalene's was reduced to the status of a chapel, then a chantry, and after the Reformation the building was converted into a town hall and school.

All that remains above ground of medieval Doncaster is the pattern and names of some of the streets. French Gate in particular evokes the memory of the Norman borough. Nothing can now be seen of the two medieval hospitals of St Nicholas (founded during the reign of Richard I) and St James (established by 1223), for they and the chapel of Our Lady of the Bridge were swept away at the Reformation. Nor are there any visible traces of the friaries of the Franciscans and the Carmelites, though their sites are known. The Franciscans established themselves in the marshy area of the Cheswold in 1284 and there were thirty friars here by the end of the century; however, the numbers had dwindled to ten by the time they were dissolved in 1538. The Carmelite friary was founded in 1351 on and near the site still known as Priory Place. The last prior, Lawrence Cook, was imprisoned and condemned for supporting the Pilgrimage of Grace and was executed in 1540 just before a pardon arrived. He had only seven friars serving under him when his house was dissolved in 1538.

Sheffield Early in the twelfth century William de Lovetot built a motte-and-bailey castle upon the ruins of Waltheof's aula at Sheffield. De Lovetot also encouraged the development of the town by building the original Lady's Bridge across the River Don, by establishing a corn mill at Millsands, by endowing a hospital on Spital Hill, and by seeing to it that Sheffield was made an independent parish with a church at the western edge of the town. The castle was destroyed by the rebels during the Barons' War of 1266, and abundant evidence of a catastrophic fire has been found during excavations. Four years later Thomas de Furnival built a massive new castle on the same site, and this dominated the town of Sheffield for nearly four centuries. John Harrison described it in his survey of 1637 as 'fairly built with stone and very spacious', and excavations have revealed a stretch of wall 21 feet high and 40 feet long, laid in courses of tooled ashlar, together with the base of an enormous circular bastion, flanked by the principal gateway and the remains of the gatehouse and the drawbridge pier. The moat on the southern and eastern sides of the castle was partly cut through rock to a depth of 30 feet. Sheffield was to remain under the dominion of its manorial lords until well into the industrial era.

Some attempt at fostering urban development appears to have been made by the de Furnivals, who had inherited the lordship through marriage. Map and street-name evidence points to a large, rectangular market place south of the castle, where markets and fairs were held from time immemorial. In 1296 Thomas de Furnival obtained a grant for a second weekly market and two annual fairs, and the following year he issued a charter to the 'free tenants of his town,' granting them certain privileges such as those enjoyed by other small boroughs. The wording of the charter implies that these free tenants or burgesses were already in existence and that their status was being recognised formally. During the fifteenth century their elected body was referred to as the Burgery; after the Reformation they were split into Twelve Capital Burgesses, who had responsibility for the upkeep of the church, and thirteen Town Trustees, who reinforced and often duplicated the work of the officials of the civil parish. The burgesses never acquired as much power as their counterparts in Doncaster, for the lord retained the jurisdictional and administrative powers of his manorial courts both within the town and throughout Hallamshire. Sheffield was one of many English boroughs of the second rank that did not achieve full corporate status during the Middle Ages. A group of burgage plots once stretched from the High Street to the present Norfolk Street, but the restrictive influence of the lord was as evident in the landscape as it was in administration; the castle sealed off the northern part of the town, and expansion beyond the Sheaf was prevented by the lord's hunting park. In the west the town stretched as far as the West Bar, and in the south it reached into Fargate and to the moor that belonged to the hamlet of Little Sheffield.

Rotherham   Rotherham and Sheffield had much in common, for each was an ancient settlement at a confluence of the Don, each had a market based on immemorial custom, and each had minor borough status. Hardly anything is known about the medieval borough of Rotherham except that a Rufford abbey charter of 1408-9 mentions land that was held by 'burgage service.' Eighteenth-century maps indicate a pattern of burgage plots to the south of High Street, and possibly also in Well Gate and West Gate, but firm proof is lacking. The monks of the Nottinghamshire abbey of Rufford had acquired both the manor and the tithes and advowson of the church during the reign of Henry III, and at the *Quo Warranto* enquiries of the late thirteenth century they claimed that their market at Rotherham had existed from time immemorial. Royal licences dating from 1207 to

1316 laid the formal bases for the Monday and Friday markets and the Midsummer and November fairs, but the monks were probably right in claiming a prescriptive origin. The market adjoined the churchyard on the south-west (though later the beast market was held on the hillside just to the south of High Street), and such a juxtaposition is a sure sign of an early foundation.

The markets and fairs were well served by the routes which converged on Rotherham's medieval bridge over the Don. Though the river course was altered in the eighteenth century, the bridge survives intact just as it was when Leland described it about 1540 as 'a fair stone bridge of four arches.' In the 1752 West Riding *Book of Bridges* it was said to be 114 feet long and fifteen feet wide. Furthermore, the chapel that was built on this

24

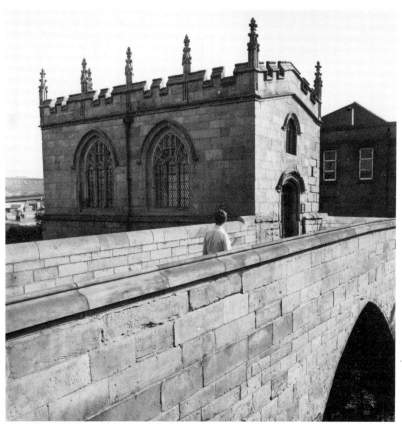

Rotherham bridge chapel is one of only five surviving examples in the country. In 1483 John Bokying, the local grammar school master, left 3s 4d 'to the fabric of the Chapel to be built on Rotherham Bridge'. When John Leland came here about 1540 he noted a 'fair Stone Bridge of iiii Arches' with 'a Chapel of Stone wel wrought'.

bridge about 1483 is one of only five to survive in the whole of England, though they were once a normal feature of the larger bridges. Having crossed the bridge, traffic could proceed along Bridgegate to the market place or up past the church and along Wellgate on the road to London. The dignified parish church was undoubtedly the glory of medieval Rotherham and one of the finest in Yorkshire. Rebuilt completely in the Perpendicular style upon the foundations of a large Norman building, it is 147 feet long and its central spire is 180 feet tall. The parish was evidently prosperous in the later Middle Ages. The south chancel chapel was built in 1480 by the town's most famous son, Thomas Rotherham, who at that time was Bishop of Lincoln, and subsequently Archbishop of York. In 1482-3 he founded the College of Jesus to provide priests to serve Rotherham church and erected what Leland described as a 'very fair college sumptuusly buildid of brike.' At the time of the Dissolution a provost, three fellows, six scholars and five chantry priests were in residence, and much of the eastern part of the town was taken up with the buildings, the extensive gardens surrounded by a high wall, and the meadows which stretched beyond.

Barnsley Barnsley also flourished as a market and communications centre. Before the twelfth century it was merely a small village and chapelry at the eastern end of the parish of Silkstone, but its fortunes were altered radically after 1156 when the manor was granted to the Cluniac priory of St John at Pontefract. The monks planted a new town half a mile east of Old Barnsley (as it was called in 1280), at the junction of the north-south route from Wakefield to Sheffield and the great highway from Richmond, Halifax and Huddersfield to Rotherham and so on to London. The new site was also much nearer the River Dearne, which may have been navigable for light craft, at least in certain sections. The showpiece of the new town was St Mary's church, which was described in the *Gentleman's Magazine* shortly before its demolition in 1820 as 'a beautiful piece of Norman work.' Nearby, the new streets of Westgate, Eastgate, Southgate, Church Street and High Street were laid out on their present lines, and a weekly market and annual fair were established in a large open space to the west of the church known as Fair Field, and also down the wide street of Market Hill.

The topography of medieval Barnsley is still clear today, but unfortunately there is very little documentary evidence to explain the pattern. Presumably, the town had its burgesses, but their existence cannot yet be proved. What is certain is that in 1249 the monks obtained a charter for an additional weekly market and annual fair, and this grant has been traditionally associated with May Day Green at the bottom of the hill. For centuries this cheerful open-air market gave Barnsley a character all of its own, but now it has been desecrated with concrete and made no different from countless other anonymous shopping centres up and down the country. May Day Green formed the southern limit of the town until the nineteenth century, and this new market benefited from the busy route which came across the Pennines and passed within easy reach of the town on its way towards Doncaster. Barnsley remained a chapelry of the parish of Silkstone, but it soon outgrew all its neighbours, for no urban competition could be found for miles around, no matter what direction the traveller took.

Bawtry Not long after the monks had planned the new settlement at Barnsley another new town was created alongside the small river port of Bawtry at the very edge of the county boundary. Bawtry lay within the Nottinghamshire parish of Blyth and was surrounded on three sides by lands that lay within Nottinghamshire, and it seems likely that the county boundary was altered so as to include the new town wholly within Yorkshire. The exact date of its foundation cannot be determined, but Bawtry is first recorded in a charter of 1199, when it belonged to a branch of the de Busli family. John de Busli's son-in-law, Robert de Vipont, was lord of Bawtry when a charter for a fair was obtained in 1213-14. The original market charter does not survive, but a market was in existence by 1247; it may have been founded before the system of royal licensing was introduced in the late twelfth century. Furthermore, a document that can be dated between 1223 and 1238 refers to the borough of Bawtry, and it is highly unlikely that the town contained burgesses but no market.

Bawtry was established as a deliberate act of town planning which was designed to take advantage of the national growth of trade and population, as were Liverpool, Newcastle upon Tyne, Salisbury, Chelmsford and many other new towns of that period. The planners diverted the Roman road from its original course (which is marked by the county boundary) into the large rectangular market place that formed the core of the new settlement. The town had a grid pattern, as did about a third of the new medieval towns throughout the country, and this pattern can still be followed along some of the street alignments such as that of Wharf Street and Scot Lane. The plan is obscured in the south-western part of the town where Bawtry Hall and the Dower House restaurant have blocked the continuation of the lines of Gainsborough Road and Swan Street towards their former junction with the Roman road, but Thomas Jefferys's map of Yorkshire of 1767-72 marks the Swan Street extension clearly. A little further north, the Crown and Posting House has blocked the extension of Church Walk, and a new entrance into the market place has been created by the turnpike road from Tickhill. The road out of the northern end of the market place swings left to Top Street, which follows the alignment of the Roman road, and then continues towards Doncaster as the Great North Road. Returning to the other end of the market place, the southern extension of the grid pattern appears to be a much later development,

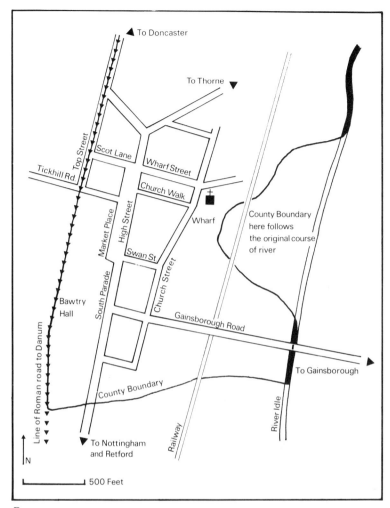

25

Bawtry.

possibly of the eighteenth century, but despite all the alterations Bawtry's medieval plan is evident to anyone who takes an observant interest in his or her surroundings. It is without doubt one of England's best examples of a new town of the Middle Ages.

Bawtry was admirably placed half-way between Doncaster and Retford, so it flourished as a thoroughfare town. Even so, it was the river traffic that was the chief concern. Bawtry was described as a port in the Hundred Rolls of 1276 and it is known that wool and lead were amongst the commodities exported two generations later. Until the eighteenth century Bawtry was the main outlet for the lead, metalware and millstones of South-West Yorkshire and North Derbyshire, and its pre-eminence as an inland port remained unchallenged until the Don was made navigable and a new canal from Chesterfield provided a direct link with the Trent.

The early topography of the place is made clear by considering the siting of the church, for as in so many towns and villages this crucial building provides a clue to an understanding of the early development of the settlement. The church is dedicated to St Nicholas, the patron saint of seafarers who has many churches in his honour in the river and sea ports of eastern England, and it is sited outside the grid pattern and cannot be seen from the centre of the market place. It stands on the edge of an old wharf which was almost obliterated by the coming of the railway in 1848; nine years later the railway company replaced their original wooden viaduct with a new one of brick and stone and they diverted the river away from the viaduct by means of a new cut. During the Elizabethan period the Earl of Shrewsbury had a staithe or wharf for exporting lead, and in 1641 a local widow said in evidence that a wharf belonging to the townsmen, known as the burgess staithe, 'butted upon the churchyard wall.' Stagnant water and lush vegetation still indicate the old course of the river and the large pool formed by the raised bank of the wharf. The view from the northern junction of the new cut and the old river course (which even now marks the erratic course of the county boundary) explains much of Bawtry's early topography, for the market place is out of sight and the church appears as the natural focal point of the wharf. Bawtry is seen not as an entirely new plantation but a small river settlement that had a town grafted on to it. The hotch-potch of re-used twelfth century material in the north aisle of the church supports the view that Bawtry was an early river port, for it incorporates pieces of Jurassic limestone and ironstone which presumably came up the river as ballast. It cannot be argued that the port came after the market town as it is inconceivable that such a large new town should have been founded without religious provision. Furthermore, as at Tickhill, some of the grid alignments follow slight curves as if they were based upon the ridge-and-furrow patterns of the open-field agriculture of an earlier settlement.

9 Roads

Water transport was far cheaper than land carriage, so wherever possible bulky goods, especially those of low value, were sent down the rivers. Only expensive items could stand the cost of long-distance carriage by land. From Bawtry goods were taken down the Idle to Stockwith and then along the Trent to Hull. Another link with Hull, and thus with London and the Continent, was provided by the lower reaches of the Don, while the Thorne boatmen worked their way up the Ouse with turf to fuel the fires of York. Throughout eastern England river ports were sited as far inland as the Great North Road. Bawtry fitted perfectly into this pattern, as did

Doncaster, where the wharf was ideally sited next to the market place.

Immemorial routes leading to the ports and the market centres can still be traced along the ground and identified by a series of distinctive place-names. The word 'road' was rarely used before the seventeenth century, for the Anglo-Saxons spoke of 'ways' and the Danish and Norse settlers referred to 'gates.' Rotherham and Darfield each have a Doncaster Gate, and the descriptive name Sandygate is to be found in Sheffield, Wombwell and Wath; Pennine villages have their Towngates, and the hazardous journey from Penistone and Langsett over the moors to the upper Derwent was made via Cut Gate. In such remote parts of the Pennines, where hamlets and isolated farmsteads often lay a few miles away from the parish church, special church-ways or kirkgates were needed to connect them. However, the majority of tracks were created for economic reasons, and some were named after the salters, jaggers, badgers and other packmen who used them.

Perhaps the most important commodity that was carried regularly over the moors to the medieval market towns was salt, which was so essential for preserving food and providing flavour. A special set of names are attached to the saltways, or saltergates as they were sometimes called, those ancient routes from the salt 'wiches' at Northwich, Middlewich and Nantwich in Cheshire, and further south at Droitwich, the *Salinae* of Roman times. The Pennine highways were used for conveying a variety of goods, but the names that are found alongside them show that the salt trade was the most important of all. Thus, Sheffield obtained most of its salt from traders who crossed the hills via Chapel en le Frith and the Winnats Pass. At Hope, a field to the south of the village was known as Salter Furlong and until recently here was a Salter Barn. Perhaps this was a recognised overnight grazing stop before the salters and their horses proceeded along Salter Lane near Bamford and over the escarpment to Stanage, eventually entering Sheffield via Psalter Lane at Nether Edge. This name was written as Salter lane in 1485, and not until the eighteenth century was the letter P added in the mistaken belief that the route was associated with the monks of Beauchief Abbey.

The most important highway across the Pennines into South Yorkshire has always been that over Woodhead. The Cheshire portion of this road was turnpiked as early as 1732, and when the Doncaster-Saltersbrook and Rotherham-Hartcliff sections were turnpiked nine years later, this ancient route was said to be 'very convenient for conveying of Goods from Eastern to Western Seas.' The first name of significance as the road emerges from Cheshire up the Etherow Valley is Saltersbrook, the boundary stream between the two counties. The modern road crosses the brook by a high bridge built about 1830, but the older track sought a much lower crossing. Then the old highway continued along a course that can be plainly followed to the horizon, both on the ground and by means of the

26

Saltersbrook, the county boundary stream, takes its name from the salters who came this way from Cheshire towards Rotherham, Barnsley and Doncaster. This ancient route was made into a turnpike road in 1741 and remained in use until the present road from Woodhead to the Flouch Inn was opened about 1830. The ruined building was formerly an inn.

Ordnance Survey map. Halfway up the hill a branch to the left heads for Wakefield along the Salterway or Saltergate that formed part of the ancient boundary between the township of Thurlstone and the Graveship of Holme, continuing through Upper Denby and along the ridgeway towards High Hoyland. However, the main highway from Saltersbrook climbed the hill in the direction of Rotherham and Doncaster until it reached the Lady Cross, an ancient and prominent landmark at a height of about 1,500 feet above sea level. Recorded in 1290 and in various boundary perambulations, it was still marked as a cross on Christopher Saxton's map of 1577, but all that now remains of it is the sturdy base and the stump of the broken shaft.

The salt track to Doncaster then continued more or less in a straight line to Hartcliff hill and then down Hillside to Hornthwaite, but in 1741 the turnpike surveyor avoided Hartcliff by a sharp detour from Fulshaw Cross through Millhouse Green and Thurlstone, The turnpike road then followed the old course through Hoylandswaine, Silkstone, Dodworth and Darfield to Doncaster, past Salter Croft at Dodworth, Saltersbrook at Goldthorpe, and Saltersgate at Scawsby. Salt names can also be located on the Rotherham route, which followed the ridge from Hartcliff to Green Moor at about 1,000 feet above sea level, past Salter Hill Farm and Plantation. After skirting Wortley along Finkle Street, the salters proceeded through Howbrook to Chapeltown and Thorpe Hesley. Here the track has been widened, metalled and occasionally diverted from its old course, but it can be traced with the aid of place names recorded on eighteenth century maps. On Fairbank's 1784 survey of the parish of Ecclesfield a Salter Close is marked at the junction with Greengate Lane in Mortomley, and on another enclosure award map the same surveyor marked a large Psalter Field of six acres and a lesser Psalter Field of 4½ acres between Hesley Wood and Thorpe Hesley, near where the saltway had reached the ridge above the Blackburn Brook. The salters then had a straightforward journey through Kimberworth and the Holmes, along Psalter Lane to the medieval bridge and the market at Rotherham. Along their route they have left the distinctive names of Saltersbrook, Salter Hill, Salter Close, Psalter Field and Psalter Lane.

The lordship of Hallamshire accounts for the mid-fifteenth century show that bulky and heavy goods were transported by oxen and two-wheeled waggons or wains. Local men were employed in this way to carry stone, timber and hay to the castle, and in 1447 no less than 120 persons with sixty wains and their draught oxen performed boon-work by carrying limestone from Roche Abbey to Sheffield. The use of wheeled vehicles in the Middle Ages was therefore not confined, as has often been suggested, to the lowland parts of England. Four years earlier, John Sayton was paid 3s 4d 'for carrying with his waggon and oxen one hogshead of salted venison from Sheffield to Worksop by command of the lord,' and then two Worksop men were paid a further 23 shillings to take the hogshead and some fresh venison by horse and waggon to London. Even in the Highland zone of the country traffic was not restricted to packhorses, and the volume of trade was sufficient to produce sunken lanes or holloways, especially on the steep hillsides. Many of the abandoned tracks that survive on the moors or in woods and fields were deepened after the Middle Ages by the traffic of the Tudor and Stuart era, and some special holloways were deliberately dug out in the eighteenth century in order to provide a regular surface and a standard width for waggons and carts taking millstones and grindstones from the quarries. Nevertheless, place-name evidence shows that some local tracks had already been worn hollow by the Middle Ages. In Derbyshire, for instance, the hamlet of Holloway, some three miles south of Matlock, had acquired its name by the first decade of the thirteenth century. Sunken tracks were also found in the towns, for Rotherham has its Hollow Gate, and in 1532 John Holland of Sheffield left 2s 0d in his will 'to the mending of Hollow Layne.'

To prevent such wear, the horses were provided with flagged paths known as causeys. These were not needed on firm surfaces but were invaluable on the sides of hills where holloways were commonly formed and over wet patches of peat on the moors. A causey is recorded at Tickhill in 1277 and another at Barnsley in 1467, but surviving examples are difficult to date for they were relaid and repaired well into the nineteenth century. Joseph Kenworthy has suggested that the series of steps that descend a hill at Upper Midhope may be identified with 'the staircase of Midhope' that formed a property boundary about 1280, but if that is so the flagstones must have been replaced, for the present ones are not worn enough to have supported 700 years of traffic. A similar stepped causeway probably accounts for the name of Stairfoot, near Barnsley, for here roads descend steeply from Monk Bretton priory and from Barnsley and Darfield. Most causeys have been replaced by better roads or are abandoned and overgrown, but the word had survived in local speech in the sense of 'causey edge' to mean a slightly-raised pavement, and has been lengthened to causeway in such examples as the Long Causeway leading to Stanage Pole.

Wherever possible the highways followed ridges high above the river valleys and the tree line, but the north-south routes had to go across the grain of the land and even the ridgeways had to cross a few key fords. The smaller medieval bridges were made of wood and not until the seventeenth and eighteenth centures were packhorse bridges built of stone. During the Middle Ages very few stone bridges could be found in South Yorkshire. The stone bridge built by 'the good men of Doncaster' in 1248 no longer survives, but a bridge of 1486 is incorporated in the present Lady's Bridge at Sheffield, which has been widened on several occasions; nothing of the original structure can be seen from on top of the bridge, but some of the medieval ribs can be seen underneath. But best of all, the 'fair

27

The Long Causeway over Stanage was a medieval highway from Sheffield into the Hope Valley. In part it followed the line of a Roman road, but this stretch is a later diversion past the pole which marks the county boundary.

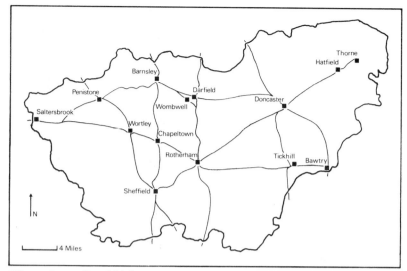

The major medieval highways.

stone bridge of four arches' that Leland saw at Rotherham about 1540 is still intact, complete with its rare bridge chapel. Eighteenth-century maps such as John Warburton's (1719-20) and Thomas Jefferys' (1767-72) show how several South Yorkshire highways converged on this bridge.

Warburton's map, which is the earliest that marks the local highways, shows that the course of our major roads (before the age of the motorways) had been determined long before the setting up of turnpike trusts. Thus Rotherham was connected by highways that followed the present routes to Sheffield, Chapeltown, Barnsley, Doncaster, Bawtry and Mansfield, and Doncaster was served not only by the Great North Road but by the present routes to Hatfield, Tickhill, Rotherham and Sheffield, Barnsley and Saltersbrook, and Wakefield. The scraps of evidence that can be pieced together from earlier periods suggest that these routes were already ancient by the time Warburton made his survey. The network of highways and byways that existed until the motor car revolutionised transport was largely complete by the end of the Middle Ages.

10 Village Markets

In medieval England there were probably three or four times as many market centres as there are today, and some of the most attractive villages in the country are in reality decayed settlements which obtained trading privileges during the thirteenth or fourteenth centuries but which never managed to develop in the same way as Barnsley, Bawtry, Doncaster, Rotherham, Sheffield or Tickhill. Hooton Pagnell, for instance, is now a classic and neat estate village built in the local Magnesian Limestone, with

The butter cross at Hooton Pagnell is a reminder of the weekly markets and annual fairs established there in 1253. Hundreds of village markets such as this came to an end during the long economic depression of the late Middle Ages.

crofts stretching from its farmsteads to the Back Lane, and with what were once its common fields and pastures reaching beyond to the prehistoric trackway that forms the eastern boundary of the parish. But a charter that is kept in the hall shows that in 1253 the local lord was ambitious to develop his village into a regional market centre, and in the village street the stump of the butter cross still stands in silent testimony to the failure of this enterprise. Similarly, charters have survived for Braithwell, Campsall, Stainforth, Wath and Wortley, all of which failed to expand, and so unsuccessful were the weekly markets and annual fairs at Scawsby and Penisale that the site of these marts cannot now be identified with any certainty.

These village markets were created during the thirteenth and early fourteenth centuries when trade was flourishing and the population expanding, but they were unable to survive the long economic recession which followed. The poll tax returns of 1379 and the lay subsidy lists of 1544 show that those villages which did not have a new town grafted on to them failed to grow naturally and were indistinguishable from the neighbouring villages. Thus, of the forty married couples and twenty-nine single persons who paid the tax at Hooton Pagnell in 1379, only two tailors and a smith were prosperous enough to be assessed at more than the basic rate. The merchants and craftsmen necessary to a flourishing market centre were missing.

The long period of steady economic growth that encouraged the

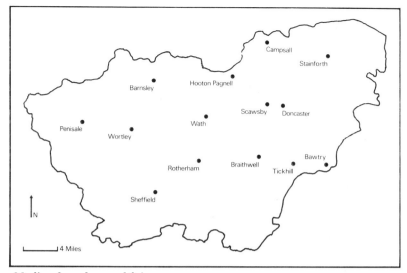

Medieval markets and fairs.

foundation of these markets was brought to an end by a succession of arable and livestock disasters between 1315 and 1322. This national crisis varied in its effects from one part of the country to another, but the consequences for South Yorkshire appear to have been severe. An Inquisition Post Mortem of the lordship of Hallamshire, taken in 1332, reveals a considerable fall in the number of inhabitants and the inability of the lord to find tenants for many of his farms. Quite clearly, the economy was in decline before the Black Death of 1349 and the subsequent epidemics reduced the national population from something approaching four million to less than 2½ million by 1400-30. Not until the Elizabethan period was the old level of population regained and it was probably during this long recession that the village markets withered away.

Fairs and markets were established in each of the agricultural regions of South Yorkshire and there is no recognisable pattern in their distribution. Individual initiative and the hostility of existing centres to the creation of new markets in their vicinity explain the choice of sites. For example, in 1293-4 Henry de Laci, lord of the honour of Pontefract, obtained charters for markets and fairs at Pontefract, Almondbury, Bradford and Campsall. The Campsall market was held on Thursdays and an annual four-day fair was arranged for each July during the festival of St Mary Magdalene, the patron saint of the church. The 1334 taxation returns reveal that Campsall men paid £7 2s 0d, the fourth highest contribution in South Yorkshire, and the 1379 poll tax returns hint at some minor trading, for a chapman (or middleman) and twelve craftsmen paid the tax, but Campsall never became more than a purely local centre. A survey of 1627 reported that 'The towne of Campsall had in tymes past the priviledge of a markett,

St Mary Magdalene's church, Campsall, has the finest Norman tower in Yorkshire. A weekly market and an annual fair were held in the village in the early Middle Ages, and Campsall parish included several hamlets on the limestone belt and in the lowlands.

which is now decayed and lost by discontinuance.' A map of about 1740 shows that the memory of the site was preserved in the name 'Market Flatt' to the north of the village where the lane from Norton joined that from Smeaton.

Few of the medieval village markets retain more evidence than their charter and sometimes the stump of a butter cross. At Wath upon Dearne the cross stood at the bottom of Sandygate at the junction with High Street until the base was removed to the safety of the vicarage garden and subsequently installed in the grounds of the Town Hall. The medieval lords of Wath were the le Flemings, and it was one of this family, Rayner le Fleming, who obtained a charter in 1312-13 for a Tuesday market and a two-day fair in September. Nothing more is known about this market, but it did not last very long. The modern market is a revival dating from 1814.

The survival of crosses long after these village markets ceased to be held has inevitably led to romantic stories about their origins. Elsewhere, township boundary stones and other crosses of unknown purpose have wrongly acquired the label 'butter cross'. The most intriguing legend concerns Braithwell, a sub-manor of the Conisbrough fee where in 1289 the local lord, Elias de Hanville, obtained a grant for a Tuesday market and an eight-day fair each July on the vigil and feast of St Margaret and on the six following days. These markets and the unusually-long fairs were held in the lower part of the village, well away from the church and the manor house, where the roads are still markedly wider as they approach the cross. The octagonal limestone base of the cross supports a rectangular shaft in the usual manner but is peculiar in having a Norman-French inscription, which Joseph Hunter complained had 'been placed [in 1798] beyond the power of any one to decypher by the blundering attempts of some country mason to restore it.' Fortunately an earlier transcript survives, and the verse is translated as 'Jesus, son of Mary, think upon the brother of our king, I beseech you.' The popular local tradition is that Braithwell was granted a fair on the first Thursday in May as a reward for paying a large voluntary sum towards the ransom of King Richard I and that the stone was erected upon the orders of King John who owned the Conisbrough fee of which Braithwell formed part. The story was current by 1798 when the inscription was re-cut and the date 1191 added in Roman numerals, and it has a superficial plausibility and enough sentimental appeal to make it widely acceptable. But it smacks of an eighteenth-century antiquarian fancy to explain something that had long been forgotten, and there are several weighty arguments that can be raised against the story. In the first place the ransom was a compulsory levy paid by all the villages in England; secondly, the bad feeling that existed between Richard and John make it unlikely that John would have commemorated his brother in this way; and thirdly, the fair was held in July, not May, and the charter was granted in 1289, not 1191. When a parliamentary survey was made of the manor of Braithwell in 1652 the surveyor made no mention of a May fair or of an 1191 charter, but noted, 'That there hath bine a Market everie weeke...and also a fayre once in the yere which hath bine of a long tyme discontinued, soe that none can remember, but that by tradition they have heard their

Anncestors say soe.' The inhabitants produced copies of the 1289 charter for a market and fair to prove their contention. The tradition linking Braithwell with King Richard I must have arisen after 1652 in an attempt to explain something that had long been forgotten, and the most convincing explanation of the stone is that it was erected by Hameline Plantagenet of Conisbrough Castle, the half-brother of King Henry II, during the late twelfth century and that it was re-used as the market cross in 1289. A similar cross was erected in Doncaster by Ote de Tilli, the steward of Conisbrough castle.

In the western part of the county an attempt to found a Sunday market at Wortley had been made in 1250, but this had been quickly suppressed by the Pontefract monks on the grounds that it harmed their market at Barnsley. This hostility was overcome two, generations later when a charter was obtained in 1307 for a Thursday market and a three-day Whitsun fair. (The main market at Barnsley was held on a Wednesday.) The market place cannot be located with any certainty, but it is surely significant that traffic on the road through the village has to negotiate two dangerous right-hand bends to pass the church. Aerial photographs show that this old ridgeway has a straight alignment as it approaches Wortley from Wharncliffe Chase and that this line is picked up again immediately beyond the bends. The most likely explanation is that the road has had to skirt the market place, which is now partly occupied by buildings opposite the church (chiefly the pub) and which partly forms the adjacent space which leads to Wortley Hall. The venture did not last long, though an attempt to revive Wortley Fair was made in the last quarter of the eighteenth century.

The history of the medieval market and fair six miles further west at Penisale is even more obscure, for the market place and fair ground cannot be identified, nor is there even any trace of a settlement. Charters show that in 1290 Elias de Midhope was granted a Tuesday market here and an annual three-day fair in June, and that these privileges were confirmed in 1307. However, the place-name was not recorded in the 1334 or 1379 taxation returns, nor can a village site be discovered either from aerial photographs or from any of the numerous vantage points on the surrounding hills, no matter what the time of day or year. Perhaps there never was a settlement here; Penisale may be a lost manorial centre with an open-air market, but not necessaily a deserted village. Tradition has it that the fairs were held near the Little Don around an old yew tree, which was burned down in the eighteenth century. Penisale fits into the pattern of open-air mid-country markets that were commonly held on borders, for the river was the ancient boundary not only of the parishes of Penistone and Ecclesfield but that between Hallamshire and the wapentake of Staincross.

One of the last places in the country to obtain a medieval charter was

Stainforth, 'the stone-ford' across the lower reaches of the Don north of Hatfield. Its Friday market and ten-day September fair were not authorised until 1348, two years after the manor had passed to the Dukes of York. Abraham de la Pryme wrote in his *History of Hatfield* in the late 1690s that Stainforth

was made a Marcket and a Fair Town by King Edward the 3rd, at the request of Edmund Duke of York, unto whom the king had given this Town amongst the Rest that belonged to the late Earl of Warren; so that this Town flourished mightily then, and became very Rich, for it had such an Advantage as few Towns had, for besides its Marcket, which was frequented by a great number of Traders, there Landed always here all those Trafficking men that came out of the Isle of Axholm, from Thorn and other Places that were every Saturday bound for Doncaster Marcket, for they never went higher up the River than this Town, and then hired Horses from thence to carry their goods thither, so that this Town was by this means as good as if it had two Markets a week. Here was sold all sorts of Wares that are usual in the Common Markets, and amongst those that were not so common, was all sorts of mill stones, grind stones, Iron ware, Lead etc, in great Quantitys, which was here carry'd off into the Idle, Trent etc. for Bautry (which is the most famous for such Wares hereabouts) was not then much frequented.

However, by 1686 the market was so moribund that Stainforth had but two guest beds and stabling facilities for only three horses. Pryme lamented, 'The town is nothing like what it was; there is now neither Market nor Fair.' The empty square where a modern market has been held within living memory is possibly the old fair ground and market place.

There may have been other village markets for which we now have neither documentary nor topographical evidence. Wombwell for instance, offers no proof of ever having had a market or fair, but in 1334 its inhabitants paid £3 16s 0d in tax, which was more than most of the known village market centres and certainly much higher than the general run of rural settlements, and in 1379 no less than sixty-nine married couples and fifty-four single persons lived there, including two knights, a chapman and twelve other craftsmen. In 1544 it remained one of the most prosperous rural settlements and in the seventeenth century it was a recognised overnight stop for the Halifax clothiers on their way to London; in 1686 it had twenty-four guest beds and stabling facilities for twenty horses. Yet it was not a parish centre and if it ever had a market in the Middle Ages it has left no evidence on the ground, nor in the records.

The long period of economic decline in the late Middle Ages not only destroyed the village markets but crippled most of the towns. Though this process is well recorded nationally, it is difficult to document it locally. We do not know when Tickhill ceased to be a borough. Continuing affluence on the part of at least some of the inhabitants is suggested by the splendid rebuilding of the tower and nave of the church during the late fourteenth and early fifteenth centuries, but by then the age of the castle and the large honour was almost over and the friary was soon to be dissolved at the Reformation. The decay probably came in the late fifteenth and early sixteenth centuries; certainly, when John Leland came this way about 1540 he remarked, 'The market town of Tikhil is very bare: but the chirch is fair and large ... Al the buildinges withyn the [castle] area be down, saving an old haulle.' Tickhill never really recovered, for it was off the major routes and did not have industrial resources; it was soon obliged to play the role of a small country market town. Doncaster must also have suffered for a time, as there was space for the Carmelites to build their friary at the heart of the town in 1351. Bawtry had declined to such an extent by the reign of Henry VIII that Leland described it as 'very bare and poore, a poore market towne.' However, it had the advantage over Tickhill of not being tied to institutions whose great age was over, and it soon recovered as an inland port, market centre and thoroughfare town once the national economy was revitalised during the reign of Queen Elizabeth.

11 Farms and Fields

Urban expansion in the early medieval period was complemented by an increase in the size of the rural population and by the colonisation of waste land. The whole of South Yorkshire was affected, but this phase of secondary settlement is observable most readily in the west, where place-names ending in carr, den, green, hey, hirst, ley, royd and wood can be found in great numbers on the Ordnance Survey maps. Permission to enclose new land from the waste was granted as a matter of course by the manorial lords, and their court rolls contain numerous references to fields that were created in this way. Just what labour was involved in clearing the land can be judged from the Sheffield manorial rolls of 1440-1 when Edward of Ryles, Agnes his wife, and Richard their son, were given permission 'to pluck up by the roots and clear away, in all lands that could be ploughed, thorns, brambles and thicket.'

Individual family enterprises such as this produced the characteristic fields of the west, those irregularly-shaped pastures and meadows that had been 'assarted' from the wastes. Such a field just north of the county boundary was cleared in 1309 when William, the son of Thomas of Hallamshire, paid a shilling entry fine and sixpence per annum rent 'to take an acre of new land from the waste of Hepworth in front of his door.' The shortage of suitable arable land called for a certain amount of co-operation between families, and in addition to their assarts each of the farmers in the Pennine hamlets had a few strips of corn in the open 'townfields'. Small hamlets had just one townfield, but the villages normally had two. During the sixteenth and seventeenth centuries many of these fields were enclosed by agreement, but others survived until the eighteenth or early nineteenth centuries. Thus, the townfields of Midhope were partitioned in 1674, but in the mid-eighteenth century Wigtwizzle

The hamlet of Rough Birchworth, 800 feet above sea level, was recorded in Domesday Book. The present field patterns preserve the outline of strips in the medieval open fields, which were enclosed by the agreement of the farmers in the seventeenth or eighteenth century.

field still contained about 120 doles or strips in seven different parts and the whole field was still farmed on a communal basis. In Bradfield a 'Nether towne fyelde' was recorded in 1590 and the open field by the church was referred to as Kirktonfield in 1416 and as le Churche Townfeild in 1558. In other parts of the chapelry of Bradfield, townfields were mentioned at Brightholmlee in 1538 and 1670, at Dungworth in 1555 and 1709, at Stannington in 1342 and 1649, and at Worral in 1701. In the neighbouring parish of Penistone the main village had an East Field and a Chapel Field, Thurlstone had an East and a West Townfield which were enclosed by the agreement of twenty-three familes in 1696, and townfields were attached to the hamlets of Carlecotes, Ecklands Hunshelf, Ingbirchworth, Rough Birchworth, Scholes and Snowden Hill, as well as at Cat Hill, High Lee, Hoylandswaine and Stainborough just outside the parish. Each of these townfields lay near the centre of a settlement in order to provide sustenance for farmers and animals in what was predominantly a pastoral area with extensive commons and wastes stretching beyond the hamlets and farmsteads.

Many Pennine farms were named after their original settlers and in turn they have given their names to the families that later resided there. The surname Bilcliff, which was once common in the Penistone area, is a good example, for it is derived from the pair of farms that stand on a spur overlooking the Little Don valley, two miles away from Penistone church. These farms are now called Upper and Lower Belle Clive but local people still know them as Bilcliff, for this was 'Billa's cliff' where a farm was in existence by the first decade of the thirteenth century. A high proportion

By the thirteenth century farmers had settled almost at the present limits of cultivation. Upper and Lower Belle Clive farms (seen in the foreground) have replaced an earlier farm on 'Billa's cliff', which was recorded shortly after the year 1200.

of West Riding surnames are derived from villages, hamlets and isolated farms, and the distribution of such names by the end of the Middle Ages shows that peasants were not tied to the manor but frequently moved within a twenty-mile radius and sometimes made considerable journeys.

Individual farms further east on the Coal-Measure sandstones have also produced surnames that are still prolific in the county. Thus, members of the Housley family originate from a woodland clearing near Chapeltown and the Blackers came from the black carr or marsh three miles further north. The Elmhirsts live at the fine timber-framed house that their ancestors built at Houndhill, only a stone's throw away from where Robert of Elmhirst was living in 1340. As Richard Elmhirst wrote in the mid-seventeenth century, 'Our Family as I conceive assumed their surname from a messuage in Worsborough-dale in the County of Yorke, which now is and for many Ages hath beene, our peculiar Inheritance, and doth not appear by any Evidence that I could ever yet see to have been the inheritance of any other Family.' The farming arrangements in this part of the country were similar to those on the edge of the Pennines. If the ancient parish of Ecclesfield is taken as an example, evidence can be found for open arable fields at Chapeltown, Ecclesfield and Wadsley (and possibly at Southey), but elsewhere the characteristic settlement was the isolated woodland farm or hamlet surrounded by its pasture closes and its meadows. During the early medieval period a great number of new farms were created as increasing population pressure forced the peasants (especially the younger sons) to extend the frontiers of cultivation in order to survive. Wilthorpe ('the wild, desolate, outlying farmstead') had been established on the wastes beyond Barnsley by 1202, and new farms in the woods gave rise to such names as Handsworth Woodhouse (by 1200), Wentworth Woodhouse (by 1303) and Norton Woodseats (by about 1280).

The fertile lands of the Magnesian Limestone belt attracted a high density of population at an early period, so nearly all the parishes were small and there was little room for settlers to set up home beyond the confines of the village. The few isolated farmsteads and small hamlets that were established were the first to succumb when the period of expansion came to a halt in the early fourteenth century. Village plans in this region have not been studied in detail, but in general expansion took the form of infilling within the villages and of a gradual extension of the open fields towards the boundaries of the parishes. The open fields of Barnburgh, for example, were extended beyond St Ellen's chapel to the ridge that forms the parish boundary, the open fields of Warmsworth stretched down to the River Don, and the cultivation terraces or 'strip lynchets' that can be seen near Thurcroft Hall and along the escarpment at High Melton brought inferior land under the plough. These changes were not spectacular but they represented the results of generations of peasant labour and enterprise.

Most of the land to the east of the Magnesian Limestone lies below the 50 feet contour line and in places is only four feet above sea level. The original settlements were mostly sited upon the banks of the rivers and several of them were small inland ports or ferrying points. The banks that were necessary to prevent flooding, such as the Sea Dyke Bank at Hatfield, could have been constructed only with communal labour. Small open fields for growing corn were attached to each of the villages, and beyond lay the low-lying meadows known as 'ings', together with the pasture closes, the extensive commons and the turf moors. Much of the reclamation of the fens and the moors was the result of peasant initiative. Younger sons were provided with land under the system of partible inheritance, so farms tended to be small and each family had to rely upon generous common rights in order to feed its livestock and to obtain timber and turf. Each township had detached pastures upon the moors, well away from the parent settlement; the inhabitants of Fishlake, for example, had grazing rights on the moors south-east of Hatfield Woodhouse, five or six miles away from their farms. The 'greens' or pastures nearest to the villages eventually attracted permanent settlers in a manner similar to the 'tyes' of Essex and Suffolk or the 'forstals' of Kent. Mawson Green and Pincheon Green near Sykehouse appear to have been settled in this way, and so do Hawkehouse Green and Kirkhouse Green near Bramwith. The economy of this region was based upon the rearing of cattle and sheep and the digging of turf, and a few minutes spent gazing at the splendid churches at Hatfield, Fishlake and Thorne provides convincing evidence of the economic success of these ventures.

Turf was important not only locally but as a source of domestic and industrial fuel as far away as York and Hull. Great advances were made into the turf moors after the Earl of Lincoln had granted turbary rights in the early fourteenth century to religious houses and other outsiders in many parts of Inclesmoor, that vast tract of land which extended from Hatfield and Thorne towards the Ouse and the Trent. Inevitably this led to boundary disputes, for property rights in this waste area had never been well defined. As Professor Beresford has shown, it was because of such contention between the Duchy of Lancaster and St Mary's abbey, York, that a map of Inclesmoor was made during the winter of 1406-7. It is now kept in the Public Record Office and is the earliest surviving map of any region in the country.

12   Deserted medieval villages

The steady expansion of the frontiers of cultivation throughout South Yorkshire came to a stop in the early fourteenth century. So severe was the subsequent prolonged recession that it took two-and-a-half centuries before there was a full recovery, and the decline in population that arrested the development of towns and market centres had such serious consequences for the smaller settlements that many of them disappeared completely. In the country as a whole, over 2,000 deserted villages have been identified. In most cases it is impossible to date this decay accurately, for many of the communities that were weakened by the economic depression of the fourteenth century did not finally succumb until their lands were converted to pasture two or three hundred years later. The Black Death rarely wiped out a community at a single blow. Sixty per cent of the beneficed clergy of the deanery of Doncaster died in 1349, but we have no means of knowing the total loss of population within the county. Later plagues and poor harvests sapped the strength of rural settlements less dramatically but just as insidiously.

In South Yorkshire deserted villages and hamlets are to be found mostly in the central parts of the county. The best example is Frickley, which was already small in 1334, and which had dwindled by 1379 to six married couples and eleven single persons over the age of sixteen. A rental of 1426 shows that the land was still farmed in the three open fields of the village, Kirkfield, Millfield and Cloughfield, but by the mid-seventeenth century all the houses had gone. Eighteenth-century landscaping has removed all traces of the village foundations, and all that now remains is the church, standing conspicuously and poignantly alone amongst the fields.

Three miles away, Stubbs Hall stands on the site of a former village,

Frickley church stands all alone in the fields, for by the seventeenth century the village that it served had disappeared. Many other medieval villages and hamlets, especially in the central part of the county, have shrunk or have gone completely.

where three carucates of land were under cultivation in 1066, and where nine married couples and seven single persons were taxed in 1379. Nearby, Deightonby and Milnthorpe have disappeared from the parish of Thurnscoe, and Bilham and Stotfold have been reduced to two or three farms within the parish of Hooton Pagnell. In 1334 Stotfold was already tiny, for its inhabitants paid the smallest amount of tax in South Yorkshire. Ridge-and-furrow patterns at Bilham confirm that what is now pasture was once under the plough. These patterns were created to assist drainage, but where they are curved like an inverted S they are also associated with the ancient strip system of the open fields. Later ridge-and-furrow patterns, like those laid down on new land during the Napoleonic wars, tend to be straight and narrow. Bilham was an early settlement, judging by its place-name, but it was one of the smallest settlements in the county in 1334 and it decayed just as certainly as did some of the later hamlets on the inferior soils. Moreover, Scawsby was founded on excellent farming land, and an undated charter in the Monk Bretton priory chartulary refers to a market that was briefly established here, but it too has disappeared as a settlement; seven married couples and thirteen single persons still resided at Scawsby in 1379, but now the site of the village is marked by a solitary seventeenth-century hall.

To the south of Scawsby most of the secondary settlements within the parish of Sprotbrough have either shrunk or have disappeared completely. In 1828 Joseph Hunter described the site of Skinthorpe as being in some fields between Cusworth and Newton, 'where there are still certain unevennesses of the surface indicative of buildings.' The name ceased to appear in taxation lists during the fourteenth century. Its neighbour, Wildthorpe, lingered on until the seventeenth century with its own three-field system but it had gone so completely by 1828 that local memory could offer no explanation for its disappearance other than it had been blown away in a violent storm! Another small township in this region now contains only the site of a moated farmstead and the earthworks of a small motte-and-bailey castle. There seem to have been two hamlets here with similar-sounding names; Langthwaite was 'the long clearing' where about 600 acres had been cleared by the time of the Domesday Survey, and Hangthwaite was 'Hagni's clearing.' The latter name gradually became confused with the former after both hamlets had been deserted. Less than two miles away a moated farmstead is all that is left of the hamlet of Tilts, and little remains of former settlements at Almholme, Shaftholme and Stockbridge. A few other minor sites disappeared in the late Middle Ages and a few that cannot be located with any certainty are known through such lost place-names as Barnthorpe in the parish of Barnburgh. Other settlements withered but did not finally die until their fields were converted to pasture in the Tudor and Stuart period. Elsewhere, villages retained their identity but were considerably reduced in size.

13   Moats and Parks

Recent fieldwork has identified about thirty moated sites within the county, and Mrs Le Patourel has shown that nearly all of them can be dated to the period 1250-1325. Few moats have strong defences and their construction seems rather to have been a matter of fashion and social prestige. One of the best surviving examples can be found just north of the church and the park at Tankersley, where it now encloses the rectory and the glebe farm; no doubt it originally surrounded the manor house before a new hall was built within the park during the Elizabethan age. Another good example is that at Moat Hall, Braithwell, the former grange of Lewes Priory. When John Vyncent of Braithwell leased the 'capital messuage called Le Priorie' in 1427 he was allowed to build 'a hall with a room to the west end 32 feet long by 18 feet broad', of which only the foundations and one arch remain. By far the greater proportion of the county's moats, however, are concentrated upon the clays and glacial drifts of the eastern lowlands, with particularly fine examples at Bentley, Fenwick, Tilts and the Radcliffe moat, which seems to have succeeded the motte-and-bailey castle as the centre of the manor at Langthwaite. Most of the moated sites are now badly overgrown and can be seen to advantage only in winter. A very fine example can be seen at all seasons, however, at a solitary farm in Thorpe in Balne on the opposite side of the

35

The moat which now surrounds the rectory and glebe farm at Tankersley probably once enclosed the medieval manor house. Most moats date from the thirteenth or fourteenth century. The road is much later and has to take two right-angled bends to pass the moat.

36

This fifteenth-century arch is all that remains above ground level at Moat Hall, Braithwell, where the monks of Lewes priory had a grange. Several monasteries acquired land in South Yorkshire and established similar granges.

river from Barnby Dun. The farmstead, outbuildings and even fishponds are enclosed by a very large moat, which appears to continue well beyond the present road. But what makes this site so redolent of the Middle Ages is the surprising discovery that the limestone barn is in fact a disused Norman chapel which still retains some original windows and a doorway, with later Gothic windows and a thirteenth-century piscina.

This Norman chapel at Thorpe in Balne lost its endowment at the Reformation and later became a barn. Set in a moated site in the parish of Barnby Dun, alongside the former manor house, it was probably founded as a chapel of ease by Otto de Tilli in the mid twelfth century. The nave was still standing when Hunter wrote in 1828, but now only the chancel survives.

Another seigneurial status symbol was a hunting park or chase. The two greatest medieval parks in South Yorkshire were associated with the castles at Sheffield and Conisbrough and may well have been created long before the Norman conquest. Most medieval deer parks, however, were created by royal licence during the thirteenth or fourteenth centuries. Grants of free warren gave lords the right to hunt in their demesne, and many proceeded to enclose a park with a ditch and an earthen bank that was surmounted by a stone wall, a quickset hedge, or wooden palings. Special leaps were contrived to allow wild deer to enter these parks but it was made impossible for them to escape. The parks were normally wooded and provided with fish ponds, for they were economic assets and not just places for sport.

Few of these parks survive in a recognisable form, but the boundaries of Tankersley Park (created 1303-4) can be followed for 4½ miles along footpaths and by the side of hedges and walls, with the aid of such place-names as Park Side, Park Gate and Warren Lane. Warrens were originally those parts of a deer park that were set aside for breeding, and it was not until after the fifteenth century that the name became associated with rabbits. The creation of this park seems to have stifled the development of the village, but unfortunately for the historian Pilley was always included with Tankersley in the medieval taxation returns, so it is impossible to

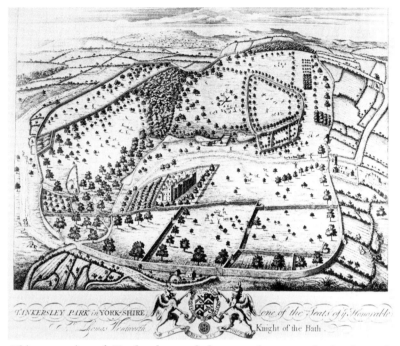

This engraving of Tankersley park by an unknown artist in the early eighteenth century shows the Elizabethan hall prior to its demolition about 1730. Note the park wall, the paddocks and the stream dammed to form fishponds. The church lay at the edge of the park but has been orientated wrongly for artistic effect.

say whether or not small farmers were driven away, as they were at Wortley when the lord enclosed his park in the sixteenth century. The Wortley family had used their grant of free warren in 1252 not to enclose a park by their village but to create a free chase upon the timbered crags of Wharncliffe. Free chases were larger than parks, and though they had well-defined bounds, they were unfenced and were usually to be found upon the manorial wastes well away from any settlement. The largest in the county was Hatfield Chase, which belonged to the de Warennes of Conisbrough castle and eventually to the crown. Seven hundred red deer roamed in this chase in 1539, and in 1607 there were about a thousand, some of which were confined to a 500-acre park west of Hatfield village. Other deer were allowed to roam throughout the countryside, and farmers sometimes had to go to great lengths to protect their crops. Old men told Abraham de la Pryme in the 1690s that in summer time the deer had once been 'so unruly that they almost ruined the Country'.

Parks were a prominent feature of the 1610 edition of Christopher Saxton's map of the West Riding at Aston, Brierley, Conisbrough,

Kiveton, Sheffield, Tankersley, Thrybergh and Wortley, and parks are also known to have survived beyond this date at Kimberworth and Finningley, which was formerly in Nottinghamshire. Some woods were also used for hunting, and according to Roger Dodsworth, writing in 1620, the de Mounteneys of Cowley manor had once had 'great woods, and abundance of redd deare, and a stately castle like house moated about, pulled down not long since by the Earl of Salop after he had purchased the land.' Cowley was a sub-manor of Hallamshire that had been granted to the Norman family of de Renneville; in the twelfth century it had passed to the de Mounteneys, and eventually it returned to the lords of Hallamshire. Other sub-manors were created within the lordship during the thirteenth century at Darnall, Ecclesall, Owlerton, Shirecliffe and Wadsley, and their lords became prosperous members of the landed gentry.

The most famous of the medieval woods of South Yorkshire was the Forest of Barnsdale, for together with Sherwood Forest is provided the setting of the earliest Robin Hood ballads, which were circulating by 1400. The 'stone of Robin Hood' was mentioned in a Monk Bretton priory

Sir John Vanbrugh designed this small folly alongside the Great North Road to commemorate Robin Hood's Well. The Forest of Barnsdale to the north of the well formed the setting of some of the earliest Robin Hood ballads.

charter of 1422, and this has been identified with Robin Hood's Well within the old forest. A small folly designed by Vanbrugh in the early eighteenth century marked this site but now stands a little further away alongside the A1. The forest had no precise boundaries, but it seems to have stretched from the district near the well as far as Wentbridge in the north. One of the earliest ballads, the *Lyttel Geste*, refers to a minor place-name, 'the Saylis', which can be located in Sayles Plantation 500 yards or so east of Wentbridge. The Great North Road came this way and the forest was sufficiently remote from the towns to make it an obvious place for outlaws. None of the attempts to identify an historical Robin Hood, however, is convincing.

14 Churches

Sites The ancient parish churches form the major collection of medieval buildings in the county, and as they have played so large a part in the life of the communities they have served much needs to be said about them here. The majority of churches were founded by local lords close to their manor houses, and those at Owston, Hickleton and High Melton still seem to be appendages of the squire's hall. Even though the church at Bradfield may have been built at a point that was fairly convenient for all the members of this moorland district, the exact site seems to have been determined by the Norman motte-and-bailey castle known as Bailey Hill. Local legend has it that the first choice of site was marked by the Anglo-Saxon cross that once stood in Low Bradfield, but that the work done each day was carried by night to Bailey Hill. This type of legend is found throughout the country wherever there was disagreement upon where to build or where a building replaced an older one on a new site. The same story is told about Penistone church and the hamlet of Snowden Hill, about Handsworth church and a site nearer Woodhouse, and about Braithwell church and the site of a holy

40

The church of St Nicholas, Bradfield, was originally a chapel-of-ease in the huge parish of Ecclesfield. Sited near a motte-and-bailey castle (obscured by the trees), it was rebuilt in the late Middle Ages.

well at the lower end of the village. High Bradfield, or Kirk Town as it was once known, never grew into anything larger than a hamlet.

In no case is the foundation date of a medieval church within South Yorkshire known to us, and the reasons for siting a building upon a particular place are often mysterious. The most intriguing site of all is that occupied by St John the Baptist's church at Throapham, or *Trapun* as it was recorded in Domesday Book. The church stands several hundred yards away from the hamlet of Throapham and only a quarter of a mile or so from All Saints, the parish church of Laughton. All Saints is obviously an early foundation, for it has an Anglo-Saxon north door and it once served the largest parish on the Magnesian Limestone. It is difficult to see how and why St John's had acquired burial rights by the time of the Normans. Throapham parish is surrounded on each side by the parish of Laughton, and St John's church is sited curiously within a small loop of its own boundary, in the middle of St John's Field, one of the three ancient open fields of the village of Laughton. The clue to the mystery has been provided by the antiquary Roger Dodsworth, who visited Throapham church in 1631. He noted that there had once been a Midsummer fair which had attracted large numbers of pilgrims to the church. Midsummer had been the occasion of a great pagan festival which the early Christians had replaced by the feast of St John the Baptist. Pilgrimages to holy places, notably to shrines and holy wells, were a common feature of Christian practice in the Middle Ages, and St Winifred's shrine at Holywell in Wales retained its semi-magical appeal throughout the seventeenth century. The well near the chancel door in Throapham churchyard may have been a similarly revered site whose heathen associations had been replaced by a dedication to the Baptist. The bonding on the south chancel wall shows that the building settled a few inches during construction; is it too fanciful to suppose this was because the church was built over a spring or well? The fair was probably held in the large field in the hamlet of Throapham that is named Chipping Croft on the tithe award map of 1841, for many market towns are still called Chipping, but Dodworth is explicit that the pilgrimage was to the church. The well, the Midsummer pilgrimage, the dedication and the extraordinary position of the church argue for such an explanation.

An interesting parallel is found at Ecclesfield, where one of the three open fields was named after St Michael's chapel, which stood in the middle of the field only a few hundred yards away from the parish church. The evidence is firmest in the case of Barnburgh, where the ruins of St Ellen's chapel lie in St Ellen's Field, the most easterly of the three open fields of the village. A remarkable number of holy wells in Yorkshire, Lancashire and Lincolnshire were dedicated to Elen, the Celtic goddess of armies and roads. The early Christians re-dedicated them to Helen, the mother of Emperor Constantine, who had made Christianity the state religion. As the letter 'h' is often silent in the Yorkshire tongue, the change was easy to accept and the name was frequently written in the old manner in local records. In addition to the wells, thirty-four Yorkshire churches are dedicated to St Helen. She ranks sixth in popularity in the shire, a ranking higher than anywhere else in Britain. Some of these churches were dedicated unequivocally to Helen because of Constantine's link with York, but those that lie near ancient roads may have had the Elen connection in mind. The parishes of Austerfield and Burghwallis were each bounded by the Roman road that passed from Bawtry through Doncaster to York, Treeton church stands near the road to Templeborough, Thurnscoe was sited upon a Roman street whose line is doubtful, and the ancient Ricknield Street served as the western boundary of the parish of Marr.

On the opposite side of Ricknield Street lay Street-flatt, a furlong in St Ellen's Field, Barnburgh. The chapel ruins have been examined and described as Norman. They are preserved in a copse a few yards up the hill from a dried-up well which is now difficult to find amongst rough ground overgrown with bushes and small trees .

An eighteenth-century Fairbank map marks another St Ellen's Field in Thorpe Hesley, and a St Ellen's Well was once found at Carlton, near Monk Bretton. The site is commemorated by the name of St Helen's Farm, which was formerly a retiring house for the priors of Monk Bretton and later a minor seat of the Wortley family. There is now no sign of a chapel, but Dodsworth noted the well, 'whither they us'd to come on Pilgrimage.' There is much that remains mysterious about early Christian practice.

Crosses Equally puzzling are the numerous stone crosses which survive in mutilated form. Once a common feature of the medieval landscape, they were mostly destroyed or broken at the Reformation. Robert Parkyn, the curate of Adwick le Street, noted that in 1548, 'Rogacion Days no procession was made about the feildes, butt cruell tirranttes did cast down all crosses standing in open ways dispittefully.' However, the villages of Maltby and Monk Bretton still have prominent crosses in their streets, and others are known from documentary sources. For example, a thirteenth-century cross, twenty feet tall with three niches for images, stood alongside the highway north of St Mary's bridge, Doncaster, until the road was widened in 1765. Elsewhere, place-names speak of the former existence of crosses; Ecclesfield has a Cross Hill, which was approached along Roods Lane, and a mile or so away a housing estate retains the name of Parson Cross. The thirteenth-century Lady Cross near the county boundary at Saltersbrook marked the border of lands granted by the lord of Glossop to the Cistercian abbey of Basingwerke. Engraved as a prominent feature on Christopher Saxton's map of the West

Riding in 1577, it survives as a stump and as a place-name well known to ramblers. Some of the crosses which are found in churchyards may have marked burial grounds and preaching stations before churches were erected, others may have been used in ritual processions, and some may simply have been moved there in recent times for safety. The St Leonard's cross at Thrybergh, which legend links romantically with a dying crusader, and which appears to be a re-used pre-conquest cross, has been moved for this reason. The base and shaft of another cross still stands in its original position nearby at the edge of Thrybergh village. Other crosses simply commemorated important individuals. A twelfth-century cross which once stood in Hall Gate, Doncaster, had a Norman-French inscription which is translated as 'This is the cross of Ote de Tilli, on whose soul God have mercy, Amen.' De Tilli was the steward of the Warennes at Conisbrough castle. His cross was eighteen feet high, with five columns capped by tall, gilt-iron crosses, but it was defaced by parliamentary troops in 1644 and was replaced in 1793 by an inaccurate substitute, which still stands in South Parade.

In addition to the crosses in Hall Gate and by St Mary's bridge, Doncaster had a famous medieval shrine to Our Lady. In 1483 Lord Rivers bequeathed his hairshirt to this shrine, and in 1537 King Henry VIII had a candle burning here. The apparently drowned wife of Robert Leche was said to have been miraculously resuscitated in front of the statue in 1525, and pilgrims flocked here until the shrine was destroyed in 1538. In June of that year Bishop Latimer wrote that the Lady Shrines at Worcester, Walsingham, Ipswich, Doncaster and Penrice 'would make a jolly muster in Smithfield. They would not be all day in burning.'

Norman churches   After the Norman conquest many new churches were erected and several old ones were rebuilt. Norman churches had thick walls and often the early ones had low, round arches and thick piers, as if the masons were frightened their buildings would collapse. Poor mortar and the use of rubble infilling meant that many of them did just that. But for the first 50 years or so native craftsmen were normally used in the smaller churches and they persevered with many features of the old style. At High Melton, the church of St James has a tall and narrow nave, with relatively thin walls, a hint of long-and-short work on the north side, and plain, unmoulded arches leading into the south aisle and the chancel, and the quoins of Maltby tower and Worsbrough chancel are laid in alternate fashion, though with stones smaller than those found in earlier buildings. Early Norman herringbone masonry was employed throughout the unbuttressed western tower at Maltby and was used lavishly at Marr and Owston and, to a lesser degree, at Brodsworth. These churches, and that at Finningley, were obviously built within a few years of each other, but in the absence of documentary evidence they cannot be dated accurately.

A small Norman church without aisles or clerestories is preserved at Adwick upon Dearne, though it is disguised by drab pebbledash and a blue-slate roof, and by lancet windows which were added in the thirteenth century. Adwick was a small parish with an absentee landlord in later times, so it was neither enlarged in the Middle Ages nor 'improved' by a Victorian squire. It has no tower, but instead it retains its rare Norman bell-cote. In 1911 Joseph Morris wrote in his *Little Guide*, 'The humble, unrestored little church is pink-washed, mouldy, and not worth a visit', but it is hard to agree with this view, for only a handful of Norman bell-cotes survive anywhere in the country. That which adorns the small Norman church at Austerfield is Victorian, and so is that at Armthorpe, whose church can just be recognised as a Norman building beneath the drastic restoration and extensions of 1885. For the full flowering of the Norman achievement one must visit Arksey and Campsall on the Magnesian Limestone belt. Arksey has a large, cruciform church built in two phases during the twelfth century, with later alterations, and its mellow stone and pleasing proportions make it one of the most aesthetically satisfying buildings in the county. About the same time as Arksey church was being built, a start was made on a cruciform church a few miles to the north of Campsall, but within a few years this plan was abandoned in favour of a western tower, which Pevsner calls the most ambitious of any Norman parish church in the West Riding. Twin bell-openings, a shafted window, a blank gallery of arches and a doorway decorated with zig-zag all combine in an effective piece of display, a striking contrast to the plain buildings that had been erected for worship in earlier times.

The present appearance of many other churches disguises the fact that they are basically Norman in character or that they retain Norman features. At Hooton Pagnell, the lower stages of the tower, the nave and its north aisle, and the original short chancel are all of the twelfth century, and so is most of St Peter's church at Edlington which recently fell into disuse and was in danger of collapse, but has now been splendidly restored by the Friends of Friendless Churches. At Wales the Norman nave and chancel were incorporated as the north aisle of a large new church in 1897, and at Wath the lower parts of the tower, the northern arcade of the nave, and the chapel to the north of the chancel are also recognisable as Norman. Other Norman work includes the towers at Finningley and Darfield, the chancel arches of at least twelve churches, and the blank arcading in the south aisle and the south porch at Wadsworth. The Normans also introduced architectural carving (as distinct from the sculptured stones of the Anglo-Saxons) into certain parts of their churches. Austerfield has an extraordinary tympanum over its door depicting a dragon with a tail shaped like an arrow, Edlington has a fine series of carved heads acting as an external corbel table on the south side of the nave and chancel, and a few

41

In Norman churches stone carvings were often placed over the entrance. At St Helen's church, Austerfield, this crude figure appears to be a dragon or serpent.

42

St Cuthbert's church, Fishlake, was rebuilt in fine style in the later Middle Ages, but the Norman south doorway was preserved. Decorated with human figures, animals, bands and leaves, it is the best of its type in Yorkshire.

buildings contain some of the finest examples of Norman art. The south door at Fishlake is the most lavishly decorated in Yorkshire, with four orders carved with animals, human figures and leaves. The font at Thorpe Salvin has richly decorated baptism and country scenes, and Conisbrough has a unique coped tomb-chest with remarkable carvings of foliage, scrolls, and figures of men and beasts, which must have been carved for someone at the castle. They rank with the best artistic achievements of twelfth-century England.

The medieval churches of South Yorkshire display few peculiar regional features, but they use local stone to blend perfectly with the landscape. In the west the sandstone towers give a sense of strength and sturdiness and the choice of site was often superb. The pinnacled tower of Penistone church, for instance, could hardly have been built in a better position to dominate the landscape of its huge Pennine parish; it acts as a landmark for miles around. But the limestone churches are the ones which

43

This remarkable Norman font in St Peter's church, Thorpe Salvin, depicts a baptism scene and the changing seasons of spring, summer, autumn and winter. Pevsner described it as 'among the most interesting Norman fonts in the country'.

44

Norman sculpture is seen at its best with this twelfth-century tomb-chest inside Conisbrough church. The carved figures include a bishop, knights on horseback, a man fighting a dragon, animals in medallions, Adam and Eve with the serpent, and signs of the zodiac.

attract the eye most pleasantly. The herringbone masonry of the lovely small church at Burghwallis effectively displays different coloured stones from a variety of local beds, and so too does the magnificent church at Laughton. Further east, in the lowlands at Hatfield local stone was unavailable, so the Normans had to use pebbles and small boulders set firmly in a mortar of lime and sand. In later times, however, ashlar masonry from the Lower Magnesian Limestone quarries was imported for a grand rebuilding, and as at Fishlake (where a short stretch of the original wall of boulders was sentimentally preserved by the late medieval builders above the priest's door), this stone sparkles in the sun and lends itself to intricate carvings.

Gothic churches   At the end of the twelfth century the Norman style gave way to Early English Gothic. Several South Yorkshire churches, notably Aston, Bawtry, Bradfield, Ecclesfield, Harthill, Norton, Penistone and Silkstone, have nave arcades that date from a transitional period about the year 1200, and straight-joints in the walls at Hooton Pagnell and Marr reveal how Norman box-shaped chancels were extended and fitted with new doors and pointed windows. A great deal of Early

English architecture survives in the chancel and chapels at Wath, but there is no church that is completely of this period in South Yorkshire. Some thirteenth-century work was replaced during later rebuildings, but elsewhere the churches erected by the Normans were deemed quite satisfactory, and all that was considered necessary was perhaps to add an aisle, fit a spire or extend the chancel and to adapt the basic structure in minor ways in accordance with the changing pattern of religious observance and the new fashions of architectural style. The continuity of tradition is pleasingly evident at Wadworth, where a spacious late Norman church has a high nave in the old manner, with aisles extended alongside the tower, as at Conisbrough and Tickhill. The arches that provide access into the aisles from the nave and tower and the entrance arches of the porches are Early English, then about 1300 the chancel was rebuilt with a fine chapel on its north side, and finally in the late fifteenth or early sixteenth centuries the clerestories and the south aisle were given new windows in the Perpendicular style and a graceful tower was built in a manner reminiscent of Sprotbrough and Conisbrough.

Few churches can be dated accurately, for they have been constantly altered and repaired, and the lack of documentary evidence makes it difficult to judge the time-span of any particular style. But during the thirteenth century narrow lancets were replaced by larger windows with intersected tracery, a style seen at its best in the eastern wall of the chancel at Penistone. The range of design that was available by the early years of the fourteenth century is apparent from the geometric patterns carved on a remarkable tomb that stands in the churchyard at Loversall. The next few decades witnessed a halt to economic progress throughout the country, yet during this period some places were able to enjoy superbly gifted craftsmen to decorate special features with ball-flower ornamentation, to carve ogee arches and to design windows with flowering tracery. In some churches the decorated style is evident only in one or two windows; elsewhere, as at Wadworth or Thorpe Salvin a new chapel might have been added, but only at Barnby Dun and South Anston are the buildings largely of the first half of the fourteenth century. The style ends with the slender, flowing tracery of the large east window at Fishlake, where the chancel was rebuilt by Richard Mauleverer, who became rector there in 1351.

The late fourteenth to the early sixteenth centuries witnessed the final phase of medieval Gothic building, known to ecclesiologists as the Perpendicular style. Most churches received no further major architectural changes until the Victorian period, so a lot of late medieval work has survived. The full recovery of much of South Yorkshire from the economic malaise is demonstrated by the size and splendour of the churches in the towns and the larger rural parishes. Most of the villages, however, were satisfied with adapting their existing structures, by adding battlements and pinnacles, replacing windows, building towers and chantry chapels, and by fitting ranges of clerestory windows. To appreciate how much the windows altered the internal as well as the external appearance of a church, one has only to compare the well-lit naves at Penistone, Sprotbrough or Tickhill with the gloomy interior at Austerfield, where the nave has a north aisle but no clerestory.

45

St Mary's church, Tickhill, is one of the glories of medieval South Yorkshire. Founded at the edge of the town in the early thirteenth century (see the tower buttresses), it was rebuilt in the Perpendicular style from the reign of Richard II onwards.

The first churches to be rebuilt in the new style were those at Tickhill and Laughton. Enough Early English work survives to show that Tickhill church had achieved its present size by the thirteenth century; a chapel was added to the north of the chancel in the 1340s, and then an ambitious rebuilding was begun late in the reign of Edward III or under his successor, Richard II. Heraldic devices on the western tower date from 1373-99, but the work was spread over many years and had not been completed by 1429 when John Sandford bequeathed £5, a cart and four horses 'to the makyng of the stepell of Tyckhill'. The striking use of ogee arches in the arcades suggests that the rebuilding of the nave was also an early venture; the chancel, too, was redesigned, but the plan to vault the inside of the tower was never completed. Perhaps Tickhill's fortunes were already on the wane, long before Leland's visit. Its church testifies to Tickhill's wealth and pride at the height of the Middle Ages; the tower ranks with the best of Somerset, and the range of clerestory windows and the unusual but effective device of having a five-light window above the chancel arch stamps it as a merchant's church comparable with the Perpendicular buildings of the Fens and East Anglia.

The contemporary church at Laughton is very different and was not the product of urban wealth. Dominated by its amazing tower and spire, which soars to a height of 185 feet, it may owe something to its peculiar dependence upon York Minster. About 1377 William of Wykeham, one of the great church builders of his age, became responsible for Laughton, and the temptation to ascribe the building to him is almost irresistible, for carved heads above the middle windows for the nave aisles are good likenesses of Edward III and Richard II and their respective queens.

Many a new tower added dignity to a building. That at Rotherham was begun in 1409, when an indulgence was granted to all those who contributed towards the cost, and the rebuilding of this fine church was completed by 1483. The tower, spire, and crossing arches at Sheffield are also of the early fifteenth century, and the old St George's church at Doncaster, which was destroyed by fire in 1853, was also reconstructed in the Perpendicular style. Rural churches were redesigned two or three generations later. At Thrybergh William de Reresby, the younger brother of the lord, was made rector, and then inherited the manor when his brother died; here then was a chance to design tower, nave and chancel in one style during the years of 1439-69. In the lowlands, the badge of Edward IV dates the proud new tower at Fishlake to 1461-83, and the arms of the Savage family on the great central tower at Hatfield suggest a late fifteenth century date for the major reconstruction of the church. Edward Savage was appointed bailiff and parker of the lordships of Hatfield and Thorne in 1485 and his brother, Thomas, became Archbishop of York in 1501. Other towers can be dated approximately from bequests in wills. Thus, in 1474 the upper part of the tower at Sprotbrough was said to be 'of new construction', and in 1497 John Skires left money towards the building of the tower of Wentworth church, which had been consecrated as a chapel-of-ease in the parish of Wath six years earlier, and which has been sadly neglected since a Victorian church was built further up the hill. In 1479 the old central tower at Silkstone was pulled down, and a new western tower was completed by 1495. At Darton, the prior of Monk Bretton had finished the chancel by 1517 and the lord and parishioners added a tower and refashioned the nave. Several other churches are so similar in style as to suggest a great deal of building activity about this time as the rural economy recovered. Royston church is almost entirely Perpendicular Gothic with all the standard elements of design, but with an unusual oriel window in the west wall of the tower to give it memorable individuality.

Interiors Internally, medieval churches once looked very different from the present appearance. Bare masonry may appeal to modern eyes, but prior to the Reformation, paintings of saints on whitened walls, gilded images and screens, stained glass windows and heraldic devices produced a blaze of colour. Fragments of medieval glass survive in several churches, notably Tickhill and Thrybergh, but apart from High Melton (where a great deal of York glass was assembled in the eighteenth century when John Fountayne of Melton Hall was Dean of York) no building can boast of much. This is unfortunate not only from an artistic point of view, but

46

All Saints' church, Darton, was completely rebuilt during the reign of Henry VIII. An inscription informs us that the prior of Monk Bretton had finished the chancel by 1517. The nave and the tower were the responsibility of the lord and the parishioners.

47

Medieval masons obviously had a sense of humour. This grotesque head supported an arch leading into a fifteenth or sixteenth century chantry chapel on the north side of St John the Baptist's church, Penistone.

because the glass depicted medieval attitudes to life and religion. Roger Dodsworth noted in 1621 that the north window in the chancel at Royston showed two angels and four oxen drawing a plough, with the inscription, 'God speed plough, And send us corne enough.'

The immediacy of the divine and the supernatural was reflected in the number of images of the saints and in the use of grotesque gargoyles to frighten away devils. The lack of early graves to the north of our churches results from the belief that this was the devil's side; indeed as late as the eighteenth century a Sheffield mob jeered and insulted a parishioner who had violated this custom. Altars to saints are referred to in numerous medieval wills. Henry of Birley, for instance, made bequests to four altars in the parish church at Ecclesfield in 1391, and it is possibly one of these altars that was converted into a tombstone and is now set in the floor of the Lady Chapel. Wills commonly provided for masses to be sung for the departed soul, and by the early fourteenth century it had become fashionable for the rich to endow chantry chapels which were usually attached to the end of the nave aisles and dedicated to a favourite saint. For example, in 1322 Henry of Eynesham bequeathed land for a chaplain to celebrate divine service in the Lady Chapel at Bolton, others were established at Todwick (1328), Owston (1333) and Skelbrook (1338), and soon most churches had similar extensions. Sometimes these chapels were far too large and ostentatious. John Wirral's chapel at Loversall is out of proportion with the rest of the building, and at Kirk Sandall the chancel is dwarfed by the chapel built by 1521 for William Rokeby, former vicar and later Archbishop of Dublin. Here is a fine monument to Rokeby, and some interesting Renaissance enamel glass. The fashion for new endowments and for rebuilding continued up to the Reformation, and the present Lady Chapels at Silkstone and Ecclesfield date from 1514 and 1533 respectively. In the chantry chapels are to be found the tombs, effigies and memorials of the leading figures of the parish. Occasionally they are of wood, like the splendid fourteenth-century effigy of a knight at Barnburgh or the gruesome Rockley monument at Worsbrough, or there is a memorial brass such as the one commemorating Robert of Hatfield and his wife at Owston, but more often the early effigies are of stone and the later ones are carved from alabaster. The monument to the fourth Earl of Shrewsbury and his two wives at Sheffield and the Fitzwilliam effigy and tomb-chest at Tickhill rank among the very best.

The fine medieval woodwork that remains in our churches ranges from several massive oak roofs to the fanciful carvings of the misericords at Ecclesfield, Loversall, Rotherham and Sprotbrough. Most of it dates from the final period of building during the fifteenth and early sixteenth centuries. Especially noteworthy are the south door at Worsbrough, the pulpits at Marr and Rossington, and the figures and inscriptions carved on the bench-ends at Ecclesfield, Rotherham, Sprotbrough and Treeton. There are also a number of fine screens, especially those at Burghwallis, Campsall, Owston and Silkstone, and several parish chests, the best of which is at Wath. The rood-lofts, however, were all swept away at the Reformation.

15   Abbeys and Priories

The history of the medieval abbeys and priories is generally recorded in greater detail than is that of the parish churches. The Cistercians were particularly active in Yorkshire and during the twelfth century they founded splendid abbeys on remote sites at Rievaulx (1132), Fountains (1135), Roche (1147), Sawley (1147) and Kirkstall (1152), and nunneries at Kirklees, Esholt, Nunappleton, Syningthwaite and Hampole. The nuns had formed a community at Hampole by 1156 and soon they received gifts of the rectories at Adwick le Street, High Melton and Marr and of estates at Clayton, Hampole, Moorhouse and elsewhere. Sixteen nuns were living here at the time of the Dissolution, but nothing now remains of the priory and Hampole is remembered best for its associations with Richard Rolle, the hermit and author of religious works, who died here in 1349. Whether or not he wrote the *Pricke of Conscience* is disputed, but this popular summary of contemporary theology is in accordance with his other mystical works, of which more manuscripts survive than those of any other medieval English writer. Miraculous cures were claimed by pilgrims

48

The alabaster effigies of George, the fourth Earl of Shrewsbury (1468-1538) and his two wives, as drawn in 1819. The finest medieval memorial in the county, it stands in the Shrewsbury Chapel of Sheffield Cathedral.

who visited his tomb at Hampole.

The setting of the ruins of Roche abbey provides one of the most beautiful and peaceful scenes in the county. Landscaped by 'Capability'

Brown in the eighteenth century as part of the Sandbeck Hall estate, the site was originally a wild one, typical of those favoured by the Cistercians. Land on each side of the stream that formed the boundary between the ancient parishes of Laughton and Maltby was granted to the monks by Richard de Busli of Tickhill castle and a minor lord, Richard, the son of Turgis. Like all Cistercian houses the abbey was dedicated to St Mary, and the special name Roche was derived from the surrounding rocks with particular reference to the one that bore some rough resemblance to a cross and which became an object of pilgrimage. The first monks came from Newminster in Northumberland, which had itself been colonised from Fountains in 1138, and the abbey was laid out on standard Cistercian lines. A generation or so after the monks first arrived the abbey church was erected. The eastern walls of both arms of the transept survive to their full height, together with some adjoining parts of the chancel walls, but the plan for the rest of the church and the nearby chapter house and monastic quarters is evident only from their foundations, for these buildings were pillaged upon the dissolution of the abbey during the reign of Henry VIII. The Cistercian order forbade the use of purely decorative detail, but the

49

Roche abbey was founded by Cistercian monks in 1147. The walls which survived the pillaging at the dissolution date from the 1170s. The setting was landscaped by 'Capability' Brown in the eighteenth century.

builders were confident in their use of the new Gothic style. The surviving parts of the church appear to date from the 1170s and rank with the cathedrals at Canterbury and Wells as the earliest examples of the Gothic style in England. The gatehouse which is partly preserved immediately below the cliff was added early in the fourteenth century. No chronicles of the abbey survive but their charters show that substantial grants of land were received over the centuries and that granges were established at Armthorpe, Barnby Dun, Bramley, Brancliffe (Notts), Dunscroft, Kirk Bramwith, Lambcote, Marr and Todwick. Up to sixty lay brothers as well as over twenty monks could have been accommodated at Roche, and there is no doubt that it was the most important abbey within the county.

The second largest monastery in South Yorkshire was the Cluniac priory at Monk Bretton, which was founded by the monks of the Priory of St John at Pontefract. About 1154 these monks received seven acres of land from a local lord, Adam Fitz Swein, in a grassy clearing or 'lound' (perhaps in the Scandinavian sense of 'sacred grove', for this is an unusual place-name in South Yorkshire) near the southern boundary of the parish of Royston, on the banks of the River Dearne. The district is still known as Lundwood, but the name of St Mary Magdalene de Lunda was gradually replaced by that of the nearby village of Bretton, or Monk Bretton as it became known. In 1281 the monks changed their allegiance and accepted the discipline of the Benedictine order. Shortly afterwards, thirteen monks were living here, and in time they acquired the tithes and other rights belonging to the churches of Royston, Bolton, Darton, Hickleton and Mexborough, as well as scattered estates upon which they established granges at Brampton, Cudworth, Rainborough (near Hoyland) and Newhall (near Laughton). The Bretton monks were also active in exploiting the seams of ironstone in their own neighbourhood. The priory was dissolved in 1538 and its sandstone buildings were plundered as effectively as were those at Roche. The church, most of the monastic quarters and infirmary are known only from their foundations but they appear to have been rebuilt or extended several times during the Middle Ages. The ruins of the south range of the rectory include two late thirteenth century windows, the gatehouse is a fifteenth-century building which incorporates twelfth-century work, the nearby administrative building is basically a late thirteenth-century structure which was altered nearly 400 years later, and there are fourteenth-century remains in the west range. Enough survives to show that this was once a prosperous religious house.

Beauchief abbey was founded by Robert Fitz Ranulph, the lord of Alfreton, about 1176 and dedicated to St Thomas Beckett. The place-name is a typical French description of a monastic site and means 'the beautiful headland', for it was then a remote clearing by the River Sheaf on the edge of the parish of Norton. Premonstratensian monks came from

Welbeck and in time this small community consisted of an abbot, twelve to fifteen canons, eight chantry priests and several lay brethren. They profited from the liberality of the lords of both Ecclesall and Sheffield and they played an important role in the development of the local economy, both in agriculture and in industry. This wealthy house was dissolved in 1537 and the solid western tower is all that now remains of the 200 foot-long abbey church and the domestic buildings. However, excavations have unearthed remains from all periods between the twelfth and fifteenth centuries.

On a smaller scale but much more intact is the fascinating priory which stands to the north of the churchyard at Ecclesfield. During the twelfth century the tithes and a rectory manor of 600 acres had been granted by the de Lovetots, the lords of Hallamshire, to the Benedictine abbey of St Wandrille in Normandy. Only two monks were here in 1325, though it is likely that numbers were higher at other times. During the 1380s, upon the expulsion of foreign monks from England, the priory and its possessions were granted to the Carthusians of St Anne's, near Coventry, and it remained in their ownership until the Reformation. The building can be dated to between 1267 and 1273, and although some restoration was necessary in the Victorian era it survives more or less intact. At the east end a two-storeyed wing includes the former chapel, which contains an east window of three lights, two smaller windows and a piscina and seat, and a small room underneath which may have been used as a cell or a study. The large wing set at right angles to the chapel was altered after the Reformation by the insertion of Tudor fireplaces and mullioned windows; the five-bay Georgian range was added in 1736.

50

Ecclesfield priory was founded by the Benedictine monks of St Wandrille in Normandy. The thirteenth-century building on the right contained a chapel and domestic quarters for the monks. After the Reformation the priory was converted into a Tudor farmhouse, and in 1736 a Georgian range was added.

Several monasteries outside the county were granted lands and tithes in South Yorkshire. For example, Rufford abbey acquired the manor and rectory of Rotherham, Lewes priory obtained extensive possessions within the fee of Conisbrough, and Kirkstall abbey received land in Bessacarr with common of pasture for 1,000 sheep and forty mares with their foals and for as many cows and pigs as they pleased. Eventually, the rectories of two out of every three South Yorkshire churches were owned by monastic houses. Amongst the granges that were established were those of Nostell priory at Barnburgh, of Kirkstall abbey at Bessacarr, of Lewes priory at Braithwell, of St Mary's, York, at Rossington, and of St Peter's, York, at Brodsworth. The sites of these medieval buildings are nowadays often occupied by substantial halls and farmsteads of later periods, but it is difficult to spot them on the map, for 'grange' became a popular name for a large house in Victorian times. The monastic granges of South Yorkshire were never as important as their counterparts in the Dales, but together with the corn mills and monastic industrial enterprises they played a significant part in the development of the local economy.

16 Industry

Documentary records of industrial activity within the county do not begin until the twelfth century, but the mineral resources of the area were undoubtedly exploited in earlier times. Orgreave was recorded in Domesday Book and its name means 'the pit from which ore was dug', and way back in the Roman period ironstone and coal were mined in the vicinity of Templeborough. The evidence is much fuller from about the mid-twelfth century onwards, starting with a deed that cannot be dated precisely by which the lord of Stainborough granted the monks of Rievaulx abbey all his ironstone, mines and minerals in Stainborough, together with woods to make charcoal. Then, in 1161 the Cistercian monks of the Lincolnshire abbey of Kirkstead were given permission to dig for ironstone on the borders of Kimberworth and Ecclesfield and to erect four forges there. The scale of the enterprise suggests that iron had been worked there previously. Part of a building erected by the monks is incorporated in the present 'Kirkstead Abbey Grange', for although the whole structure was extensively restored in 1900, some Norman and early Gothic features can still be seen. Elsewhere in the western half of the county, the old form of the place-name Brightside was recorded in 1171 and means the 'smith's hearth'. Ironstone mines were being worked at Barnsley in 1284, 'orepittes' had been sunk at Pitsmoor by 1315, and the monks of Beauchief abbey were mining ironstone at Greenhill and Norton in the thirteenth and fourteenth centuries.

Other people too, lords and peasants alike, supplemented their profits or earnings from farming with incomes from industry. In 1268 the

51

Since its restoration in 1900 this remarkable building near Kimberworth has been known as Kirkstead Abbey Grange. In 1161 Kirkstead monks were allowed to dig for iron ore nearby and to erect furnaces and forges. The building incorporates Norman windows and doorways and two small Gothic windows.

Furnivals had smithies in their park and in the woods of Hallamshire, and the surnames of contemporary local men show that many of them were smiths, nailers or cutlers. The 1379 poll tax returns record metalworkers in several places, and Chaucer's reference to the Sheffield 'thwitel' or knife borne by the Miller of Trumpington shows that local cutlery had a national reputation by the end of the fourteenth century. The skilled craftsmen were mostly townsmen, while the rural metalworkers were part-time farmers, as in later times. The reference to a scythe-mill at Holbrook in 1489 suggests that the district immediately south of Sheffield was possibly already specialising in scythes and sickles, and the signs are that the industry was well established by the late medieval period. When John Leland visited the county about 1540 he wrote, 'Ther be many smithes and cuttelars in Halamshire . . . in Rotherham be veri good smithes for all cutting tools.'

The earliest references to coal mining in South Yorkshire are contained, ominously, in the records of two inquests held during the reign of Edward I. In 1293 a man met his death while digging coal near his home at Bull Haw, Silkstone, and about the same time two other men were killed in a small pit near Masbrough. Four deeds dated between 1370 and 1388 are the next source of information. They relate to two shallow pits on the outcrop of the Barnsley seam. In 1370 Thomas Toy, Robert of Denby and Robert Benet agreed to pay £5 per annum and a levy of sixteen loads of good coal a year for the lease of Sir John Fitzwilliam's pit at Cortworth, near Wentworth, which they were to open at their own expense. The last deed of the series granted the Fitzwilliams 'all the mine which was beneath two acres of land' in nearby Nether Haugh. The famous Silkstone seam, which outcrops further west, was being worked about the same time, for a deed of 1397 mentions a 'colepitte' in Silkstone. But no doubt the history of mining in the area is much older than the chance survival of documents would suggest. Leland was surprised to find that so much coal was consumed in a woodland area: 'Though betwixt Cawood and Rotherham be good plenti of wood, yet the people burne much yerth [ie earth] cole, bycawse hit is plentifully found ther, and sold good chepe. A mile from Rotherham be veri góod pittes of cole.' He further noted that 'Hallamshire hath plenti of woodde, and yet ther is burnid much se cole.'

As nearly all medieval domestic buildings were timber-framed, relatively few masons were required. The 1379 poll tax returns record fifteen masons, three slaters and a waller scattered throughout the county who were prosperous enough to be taxed at a higher rate than most. But though masons were few in the Middle Ages, one type of local stone had already acquired a national reputation. The beautifully milky white or pale yellow stones of the Lower Magnesian Limestone levels were transported from local quarries down the rivers and along the coast to be used in some of the finest buildings of eastern and southern England. Marr stone was used for heightening the walls of Westminster Hall in 1395 and was mentioned in royal manorial accounts half a century later, and when the porches of King's College, Cambridge, were built in 1513, the mason was instructed to provide 'good sufficient and noble stone of Hampole quarryes in Yorkshire.' The same type of stone had been used locally in the late twelfth century for building Conisbrough castle and Roche abbey, and was used in all the medieval churches of the eastern half of the county.

The poll tax returns show that most villages had a few specialist craftsmen, particularly smiths, cobblers, and those working with wood or textiles. The numbers recorded are minimal ones for only those wealthy enough to pay more than the basic rate were listed according to their trade, and some managed to avoid paying altogether. Nevertheless, at least sixty wrights and as many as 106 tailors were recorded in fifty-seven different places and the textile crafts were scattered much more widely than in later times, with forty-nine weavers, twenty-five fullers, sixteen drapers, four shearmen and three dyers. About half of the fullers and twenty-seven of the weavers lived in the eastern half of the county in 1379, and even as late as 1554 Doncaster, Laughton, Loversall and Wadworth were included in a list of places where woollen cloth was made. Doncaster and Sprotbrough had fulling mills, and a prominent part of Doncaster market place was assigned to the drapers' stalls. In the west, fulling mills were in operation near Dore by 1280, in Hoyland before 1290, at Oxspring by 1306, and at several other places. The trade flourished in South Yorkshire until the early years of the Industrial Revolution and helped to pay for some of the fine halls that were erected during the sixteenth and seventeenth centuries.

17 Houses and Barns

The stone houses and farm buildings of South Yorkshire fit so well into the present landscape that it is difficult to visualise the area without them. In fact they are rarely more than 300-400 years old. It is true that some Norman masonry is incorporated in 'Kirkstead Abbey Grange' near Kimberworth, that early Gothic work is evident in the Friary at Tickhill, and that a thirteenth-century sandstone priory forms an integral part of Ecclesfield Hall, but these buildings are exceptional in having been associated with religious houses. The characteristic domestic architecture was timber framed, and although slates were used for roofing, and rubble for foundations and plinths, few houses were built wholly of stone. Thus, when John Leland visited South Yorkshire about 1540 he found that 'The hole toune of Doncaster is builded of wodde, and the houses be slatid: yet is there great plenty of stone there about.' Magnesian Limestone was used for the fourteenth-century gatehouse at Hooton Pagnell Hall, for the fifteenth-century manor house that has been adapted as a vicarage at Campsall, and for a former stone house at Marr, whose ruins were described by Hunter, and both sandstone ashlar and wood were used in the courtyard house known as Denaby Old Hall, but most people found that

52

The Old Vicarage at Campsall was originally the fifteenth-century manor house, with new windows inserted about 1800. It is a rare local example of a stone-built medieval house. Internally, it retains its original roof and the doorway and window of a chapel.

53

The ruins of Sheffield Manor Lodge, as depicted in S.H. Grimm's water colour of about 1790. The lodge was begun about 1525 for George, the fourth Earl of Shrewsbury and lord of Hallamshire. Cardinal Wolsey and Mary, Queen of Scots both stayed here. Most of the lodge was demolished in 1706, but the plan of the building is being recovered by excavation.

whereas timber was still plentiful locally, the cost of working and transporting stone was prohibitive. This was true not only of South Yorkshire but of England as a whole.

Sheffield Manor Lodge was one of the few domestic stone buildings in the west. Most of the building has been demolished, but enough masonry survives to demonstrate the original plan, with an inner courtyard, long gallery, and the northern tower where Cardinal Wolsey stayed in 1529 upon his fall from power. Begun in about 1525, when it was becoming fashionable to build a country house inside a park, it was to be one of the prisons of Mary, Queen of Scots between 1570 and 1584. The three-storeyed turret house, which survives intact to the south of the main building, must have been erected about the time of Mary's imprisonment. Most of the lodge was dismantled in 1706, but its story is gradually being pieced together by the team of archaeologists who have been working on the site over the last few summers. An unusual feature of the building was the brickwork of the two polygonal turrets that stood at each side of the main gateway. Brick had been used from the fourteenth century onwards in the grander buildings of Hull and Beverley but was rarely employed in South Yorkshire before the seventeenth century. The only other brick building that is known to have been erected here in medieval times was the College of Jesus that Archbishop Rotherham founded in 1482-3. At the time of writing, the original brick walls that are hidden behind the facade of the former *Old College Inn* are threatened with demolition to make way for a new Woolworth's departmental store.

Most of the surviving timber frames are hidden from view, encased in stone or brick of a much later period. Often they can be seen only from the inside. This is especially true of cruck-framed buildings, which are to be found in great numbers in South-West Yorkshire and North Derbyshire. Despite the fact that many have been demolished since Addy and Innocent wrote their pioneer studies, it is still probably correct to say that no other area of a comparable size has quite so many. Crucks are found in the Highland zone of Britain and in parts of the Midlands, but they are absent altogether from Eastern and South-Eastern England. Mr Peter Ryder has compiled a list of over 150 South Yorkshire examples that are either still standing or are known to have been demolished during the present century, but apart from one cruck blade that has recently been found in a house at Braithwell none exists on or to the east of the Magnesian Limestone. On the other hand, the early fifteenth-century map of Inclesmoor has a drawing of a ground-floor cruck at Hatfield and of a full cruck-framed house further east at Hook, and it remains an open question as to whether crucks were always rare in the Lowland zone or whether they were an early feature that has since disappeared.

The South Yorkshire crucks are between one and six bays in length and are nearly all of a simple, distinctive type. The county has few of the varieties of style that are to be found elsewhere. The timbers are sturdy and often rough, and those at Tom Hill barn, Dungworth, still have some of their bark upon them. Carpenters' marks show that timber frames were assembled at the site. Holes were drilled near the base of the blades and poles thrust through them so that, with the aid of ropes, the timbers could be lifted onto stone footings. A few crucks were raised several feet in this way, but the great majority were raised only the few inches that were

54

This cruck frame at Dyke Side, Langsett, was revealed when the building was demolished early this century. Many such frames survive in the western part of the county, particularly in barns, but they are invariably hidden from view behind later walls.

necessary to prevent the timbers from rotting, and the frames in the barns at Concord Park and Hall Broom Farm rest simply on paving stones or upon a foundation of rubble. There were no standard procedures for constructing a frame; South Yorkshire carpenters used nine different methods of fixing the ridge pole onto the top of the cruck blades, and in a few cases they used two methods in the same building. Similarly, the distance between two pairs of crucks varied not only from barn to barn but often from bay to bay within a barn.

When a cruck frame was encased in stone, the old wattle-and-daub walls were usually removed. Some of the plaster and the laths can still be seen between the collar and the upper-tie beam at the western end of the barn in Concord Park, and sockets remain in other beams where the laths have been removed. In this particular example the rafters have also been replaced, most of the wind-braces have gone, and in order to create extra space each of the lower tie-beams has been removed. The wall plates were also made redundant when the building was encased in stone, and most of them have been taken away. Most barns have been altered in similar ways. Another interesting example is a barn of six bays at Green Farm, Stocksbridge, which has three inscriptions on its outer walls to show that the stonework was the responsibility of William Couldwell and his wife, Sara, in 1688. It is quite evident from the inside that the cruck-frame is older than the stone shell, for new purlins had to be added to alter the pitch

55

A cruck barn at High Storrs, Sheffield, now demolished. This engraving was made by James Moore, who was active locally in the mid 1880s. The tie-beams which joined the cruck blades together half way up have been cut away to provide extra space after the original walls had been rebuilt in stone.

of the roof and to make the barn a little wider.

The lack of decorative detail on the timbers makes it impossible to date these buildings accurately. The most that can be said is that although the method of construction is an ancient one the majority of surviving crucks were erected sometime between the fifteenth and the seventeenth centuries. In parts of Scotland crucks were still being erected during the late-eighteenth century. Most of the surviving South Yorkshire frames are probably medieval, for oak must still have been plentiful when their heavy, robust timbers were assembled. But cruck frames were still being constructed locally as late as 1638, when Hugh Mellor, a yeoman-cutler of Shiregreen, bequeathed unto 'Hugh Mellor my second sonne two paire of Crookes Allredie broken, one longe piece of timber unbroken, two long poules or peices towards the building him of a Smythey', with 'Twenty shillings towards the Workmanshipp thereof.' A demolished cruck-framed building from Waleswood has been dated by its tree rings to 1630-40, and a cruck at Hangram Lane Farm, Fulwood, has been dated by a similar method to the 1540s.

Crucks were held low in social esteem and their use was abandoned early in all but the smallest dwellings, barns and outhouses. Less than one-fifth of the local examples were found in houses or cottages and very few barns and outbuildings contain evidence in the form of fireplaces or smoke-blackened beams to suggest that they served once as habitations. As early as 1474 crucks were regarded as unsuitable for the more substantial dwelling houses, for in that year a lease of property at Rawmarsh provided for a new cruck barn of five bays but specified that the dwelling house was to be framed in a different style with ten posts. Similarly, Swaithe Hall, near Worsbrough, and a farmhouse in Hatfield House Lane, Sheffield, were each built with upright principal posts but their barns were framed with crucks.

The largest medieval barns were built in the aisled-hall style that was popular in the West Riding and which can still be recognised in a few houses. The two finest timber-framed barns in South Yorkshire are in this tradition. The Long Barn at Whiston is of national importance in that it is one of the few secular buildings that survive from so early a date; judging from its carpentry techniques it appears to have been constructed possibly as early as the thirteenth or fourteenth century. At the time of writing, the stone shell is badly in need of repair but the nine bays of timber framing are in a reasonable state of preservation. The other barn has recently been restored and is in excellent condition. It stands in the Viking clearing of Gunthwaite in a remote part of the ancient parish of Penistone and is approached by a long, stepped causey. Even though the hall has long been demolished, few places are so redolent of the Middle Ages. The barn dates from about 1500-50 and is undoubtedly one of the finest in the country; 165 feet long, it is divided into eleven bays by wooden posts which

The Long Barn at Whiston was erected in the thirteenth or fourteenth century and extended in the late Middle Ages. The barn is undoubtedly of national importance, but the later walls and roof are in poor condition and its future is uncertain.

The magnificent sixteenth-century barn at Gunthwaite is eleven bays long and still fulfils its original purpose, though it now serves two farms. Few places have such an immediate appeal as this.

are fourteen inches wide and nine inches thick. The floor area covers about 7,100 square feet and now provides storage space for two farms. Sandstone is used for the lower walls, but above the bressumer are large timbered panels, which on the side nearest the hall are decorated with those herringbone patterns that used to delight the eyes of Yorkshire people. King-posts support the roof, and the carpentry techniques are more advanced than at Whiston.

These two barns are outstanding, but smaller structures of a similar type can be found hidden inside later stone or brick walls. Shore Hall Farm barn, near Penistone, has a post-and-truss frame of four bays with aisles, but without king-posts; after the Middle Ages it was extended and given stone walls and a slate roof, but the timber frame is fourteenth or early fifteenth century. A similar barn stands at Nether Haugh, and two timber-framed barns in the farmyard at Falthwaite are well preserved and still used; the one nearest the farmhouse originally had an aisle, but the other is aisleless and has a king-post roof, so is probably later.

A wealth of medieval building survives in South Yorkshire, though much of it is not immediately apparent to the casual eye. For instance, the older part of Green Farm, near Stocksbridge, at first sight appears to conform with the 1718 datestone over the main door, but a recent investigation, prompted by the threat of demolition, has revealed a late-medieval timber framed house consisting of an open hall and chambered wings, with a cross-passage separating the hall from the service end. The building does not have aisles but otherwise resembles the aisled-hall construction with upright principals, king-post trusses and sturdy timbers throughout. Here is a house that stands comparison in design and carpentry techniques with most parts of England. Yet it was erected on the edge of the Pennines, 850 feet above sea level, in what historians have regarded as one of the poorest areas of the country. How the owner obtained his wealth we do not know, but the building does not seem to have been a monastic grange. The associated cruck-framed barn is six bays long, so the farm must have been a large one; the barn was presumably used mainly to store hay and to provide winter quarters for livestock, for otherwise little but oats could have been grown with such thin soils and a harsh climate. Cattle and sheep rearing must have been the mainstay but extra wealth may have been obtained from the textile industry. Even as late as the eighteenth century clothiers flourished in this area.

We are still in the dark about many aspects of medieval life, but patient documentary research and detailed fieldwork surveys are beginning to challenge many accepted notions. The idea that South Yorkshire was a backward area in the Middle Ages and, indeed, that it remained so until the Industrial Revolution is one that simply does not convince anyone who is prepared to use his eyes. Sometimes medieval houses are tucked away in rural hamlets and are disguised by later walls and extensions. Barbot Hall, Harley Hall and Swaithe Hall can be recognised once they have been found, but the medieval Court House at Midhope is used now for animals and is disguised by eighteenth or nineteenth-century walls; miraculously, the hay-loft preserves a fourteenth-century window which once looked out to the south and gave the building a decidedly superior air.

The wooden buildings that Leland noticed in Doncaster have all gone, but the former Three Cranes in Rotherham High Street has timber-framed gables, and a king-post is visible to the rear of a shop in Church Street, Barnsley. The skill and taste of local carpenters is displayed by three late-medieval houses that can still be seen in Sheffield. Each has close upright posts set into a stone sill, with attractively carved and slightly-jettied gables and king-post roofs. At Broom Hall just one wing of the Wickersleys' family home has survived William Jessop's conversion of the building into an H-plan sometime between 1580 and 1630 and the alterations of the eighteenth century; it is now almost hidden from public view. Near the centre of the town, the Queen's Head retains its original exterior in an incongruous setting alongside the bus station; it was known formerly as the 'Hall in the Ponds' and must have been rather isolated in this low-lying area. But the finest of the three houses is the so-called Bishops' House at Norton Lees, which has recently been restored as a folk museum. The Blythe family were resident in this district from at least the reign of Edward III, and one of their members probably built the original house about 1500. This consisted of a central open-hall with a kitchen to the east and a parlour and buttery, chambered over, in the wing to the west. The house was altered and extended during the seventeenth century when the Blythes were yeomen farmers and organisers of the scythe trade, but in

58

The rear gable of Ashley Jackson's shop in Church Street, Barnsley, shows that the building is timber-framed with the usual king-post arrangement. Many similar frames elsewhere are hidden from view behind later stone or brick walls.

59

The Queen's Head, Sheffield, as it was engraved for the Gentleman's Magazine *in 1821. Now a public house alongside Pond Street bus station, this late-medieval timber-framed building was formerly known as the Hall in the Ponds.*

60

Bishops' House, Sheffield, as shown in Edward Blore's drawing of 1823. Now a folk museum, this late-medieval yeoman's house has many of the characteristics of the timber-framed buildings of this region.

external appearance it remains a delightful example of a late-medieval domestic building and one of the most pleasing reminders of the Middle Ages.

From the Reformation to the Civil War

18 The Reformation

The second half of the reign of Henry VIII was a period of dramatic change at both the national and the local level. During that time the authority of the Pope was rejected, the great abbeys and priories were dissolved, the endowments of the chantry chapels were confiscated, and the pattern of landholding was transformed. The immediate consequence was rebellion, for within months of the closure of the first abbeys in 1536 the revolt known as the Pilgrimage of Grace had erupted in the north. But the way to the capital was barred by the royal stronghold of Tickhill and by George Talbot, fourth Earl of Shrewsbury and Lord of Hallamshire. Without Talbot's support the rebels had no hope of further advance and the revolt petered out after the signing of an uneasy truce at Doncaster.

Beauchief abbey was dissolved in 1537 and Monk Bretton priory and Roche abbey were closed in June 1538. Upon the rejection of the nineteen monks at Roche the whole neighbourhood took part in an unseemly scramble for plunder. The son of an eye witness wrote in 1591, 'All things of price [were] either spoiled, carped away, or defaced to the uttermost . . . it seemeth that every person bent himself to filch and spoil what he could . . . nothing was spared but the oxhouses and swinecoates and such other houses of office, that stood without the walls.' The timber was sold to the local gentry and yeomen (except for the choir stalls, which were burnt in order to melt the lead in the roofs) and most of the freestone was taken away in carts. The smaller priories at Hampole and Ecclesfield were dissolved in 1539, and the Order of the Knights of St John of Jerusalem was abolished the following year. The knights owned manors at Swinton and Hoyland and had property scattered elsewhere in the county. Their lay successors continued the tradition of marking their buildings with crosses, such as those that can still be seen on the corbels of Platts Farm near Bradfield.

The confiscation of ecclesiastical property was completed in 1546 when Henry seized the endowments of the chantry chapels. Dr R.B. Smith has shown that before the Dissolution religious bodies owned nearly a fifth of the freehold land of that part of South Yorkshire that lay within the wapentake of Strafforth and Tickhill and over a quarter of the freehold land of the wapentakes of Staincross and Osgoldcross. Most of this property came onto what was already an active market in land transactions, and men with the resources to expand were able to benefit accordingly. Thus, to quote but a few examples, the Strelley family acquired much of the former Beauchief abbey estate; the Wortleys bought the Monk Bretton prior's retiring house at Carlton; Hugh Wirral, the son of a Doncaster merchant, added Carr House, the former Monk Bretton priory grange at Greasbrough, to the property his father had bought over the years in Loversall, Stancil and Tickhill; and the Earl of Shrewsbury obtained all the lands of Rufford abbey, including the manor of Rotherham. By the end of the sixteenth century most of the land that had belonged to the dissolved religious bodies had been acquired by the local nobility and gentry.

19 The Gentry

The Talbots, Earls of Shrewsbury, normally resided in their manor lodge at Sheffield and during the sixteenth century were undoubtedly the most powerful family in South Yorkshire, and one of the most famous in the land. The other major lordships belonged to the Crown, for the honours of Tickhill and Pontefract formed part of the Duchy of Lancaster, and the fee of Conisbrough had come under royal control in 1461, when Edward IV became king of England. But just over half of the freehold land in South Yorkshire was owned by the gentry. Most of these gentlemen were lords of small manors, and although no one man could dominate a large area, collectively they were of the greatest importance. Many families could trace their ancestry back to the medieval knightly class, and the Rockleys, Wentworths and Wortleys had taken their surnames from their place of residence. Their style of living was similar to that of the Mounteneys of Cowley, who had extensive woods for hunting deer, a 'stately castle like house moated about', the patronage of a chapel-of-ease nearby at Chapeltown and a second moated house just up the hill at Hesley. Families like the Bosvilles of Gunthwaite and the Sandfords of Thorpe Salvin had been minor lords for several generations, but there were also newcomers to the area, like the Copleys of Sprotbrough and the Darcys of Aston, and opportunities for men like Stephen Bright of Carbrook or the Cutlers of Stainborough to rise to the coveted rank of gentleman. Although the local gentry were much inter-related they were not a tightly-knit class and the range of wealth was considerable. The most enterprising exploited their mineral resources, improved their farming methods, enclosed some of the wastes, and increased their revenue by allowing tenants to convert customary land into leasehold property. Their prosperity enabled them to build those splendid halls that are still such a feature of the western part of the county.

Some of these families were ruthless in their use of power. For instance, Sir William Gascoigne, the wealthy lord of Burghwallis, intimidated the lesser lord of Carcroft, who refused to accept that his property came under

Gascoigne's jurisdiction. In 1530 Gascoigne's men attacked the lesser lord in Norton chapel and took away his cattle. When the case was brought before the justices of the peace, a hundred of Gascoigne's men prevented a fair hearing, for few dared to oppose such a lord in his own neighbourhood. Another act of aggression occurred in 1524, after complaints at the manor court of Thurlstone that Holmfirth farmers, 'having recently taken their own common', were driving their cattle onto the common land of Thurlstone. Such disputes were inevitable in a moorland area where boundaries were ill defined. The issue was resolved violently. When Robert Mokeston took his turn to watch and tried to drive away the encroaching cattle he was beaten so badly that within a few days he died. Sir Richard Tempest was able to get a verdict of 'Not Guilty' for his tenants when they appealed to him at Sandall castle, but the Thurlstone men had an equally powerful protector in Sir Henry Savile. The case was taken to the Court of Star Chamber, but the verdict is not known.

The exploitation of power by three members of the Wortley family is worth considering in detail for it illustrates many aspects of life in the sixteenth and seventeenth centuries. In 1252 the Wortleys had obtained a grant of free warren with which to create a hunting chase on Wharncliffe Crags. During the reign of Henry VIII this chase was extended in a most brutal manner by Sir Thomas Wortley. The traditions are confused, but there is no doubt that some small freeholders were ejected and that the hamlets of Stanfield and Whitley were violently depopulated. In 1510 Sir Thomas built a hunting lodge on a most splendid site on the top of the crags, and about the same time he built a hall at the edge of the village of Wortley and laid out a park in front of it.

The Old Park, as it became known, did not achieve its final form until 1589. It also seems likely that the New Park that was enclosed by Sir Richard Wortley at the Grenoside end of Wharncliffe Chase was created during the reign of Elizabeth for in the 1590s this was the scene of violent events. In the Court of Chancery it was alleged that during the night of 26 October 1591, Gilbert Dickenson of Barnes Hall, William Dickenson, senior and junior, William and Ralph Broomhead, and John Street hunted deer in Wortley Park with dogs and bows and arrows. They were also charged with shooting at Sir Richard Wortley's bull and with breaking the pales, stoops and rails in Howbrook Lane. A further series of charges was preferred both against these defendants and against Christopher and Richard Wilson, John Syver, Philip Ashbury and George Blount. They were said to have entered Wharncliffe Chase on the night of 11 December 1591 and to have overthrown two great stone walls near Stead Springs Side and White Carr. A month later, on 15 January 1592, they were further alleged to have been involved in some rough horseplay which appears to have had satirical overtones. Having killed a deer in the park, they hung the flesh upon gallows and attached a deer's head and a libellous inscription to the church porch at Wortley. The following month they again destroyed the wall at Stead Springs, where Wharncliffe Chase bordered the parish of Ecclesfield.

The Wortleys were supported in the case by Richard Lord, vicar of Ecclesfield, who claimed that Gilbert Dickenson and the two Broomheads were 'persons suspected for many disorders and misdemenours', so that his parishioners were frightened of offending them. He produced an astonishing list of alleged crimes, including the killing of his tithe lambs, cutting off the tails of his horse and mare, hanging horses' heads and other bones on poles, mowing flax at night before it was ripe, wringing the necks of geese, cutting sheep to pieces, wrecking ploughs and yokes, breaking walls and killing dogs and swine. They were the terror of the neighbourhood. And yet Gilbert Dickenson was granted a general pardon in 1605, and however violent was his behaviour he seems to have claimed some justification for his brutal actions. It is significant that at least some of the atrocities were directed against the tithe system and against the enlargement of the park. The chief enemies of these villains were an unscrupulous knight and a vicar, and the hooliganism was at least partly infused with a sense of justice.

Their struggle has been immortalized by the seventeenth-century satirical ballad, *The Dragon of Wantley*. The dragon is identified plainly with the lord of Wortley; 'In Yorkshire, near Rotherham, the place I know it well....' The ballad draws upon the earlier traditions of depopulation at the time of the first extension of the chase as well as upon the events of the 1590s and it contains a clear reference to the way in which the Wortleys destroyed farms and settlements on Wharncliffe.

> All sorts of cattle this Dragon did eat:
> Some say he eat up trees;
> And that the forest sure he would
> Devour by degrees;
> For houses and churches were to him geese and turkies,
> He eat all, and left none behind;
> But some stones dear Jack, which he couldn't crack
> Which on the hills you will find.

The ballad contains nineteen verses, each of eight lines, and is based upon the stories of Hercules or of St George and the dragon. Its hero was a man who resisted all attempts to devour him and who eventually destroyed the beast (to use the direct language of the satirical ballad) by a mortal kick up the arse.

> But Moore of Moore Hall, with nothing at all,
> He slew the dragon of Wantley.

More Hall is a farmstead just across the River Don from Wharncliffe Chase in full view of the hunting lodge or 'Dragon's Den'. Its occupant at the time of the troubles in the 1590s was George Blount, who was one of the men charged with Gilbert Dickenson in 1594. Blount clashed on another occasion with Sir Richard Wortley over some lands that he owned in the neighbouring parish of Penistone, where Wortley was farmer of the tithes. In 1603 Wortley tried to increase his profits by demanding tithes in kind instead of receiving the customary small payment. Blount refused to accept these demands and after a long struggle eventually won his point. The fearsome dragon had been defeated.

Sir Richard's successor, Sir Francis Wortley, rose equally roughshod over the feelings and rights of less powerful men, and provoked as much opposition. Thus, when he enclosed part of the commons of Hoylands-waine in April 1629 thirteen men 'armed and arraied with swordes daggors pitchforkes pikestaves axes spades and other weapons' met at night time 'in forcible and warlike manner' and destroyed the new hedges and ditches. But such desperate action was always defeated by the process of law.

During the reigns of Elizabeth and the early Stuarts some of the old deer parks were changed in significant ways. In 1575 the timber in Conisbrough Park was felled and sold to local men for £1,900, coal pits and ironstone mines were sunk in Sheffield Park, and in the 1570s flower beds and a central path were laid out in front of the hall at Wentworth Woodhouse. Richard Marris, the steward at Wentworth, wrote in 1633, 'I have planted 150 trees that came out of Holland and twice as many more of Elms and birks and others which I hope will please your Lordship when they florishe on the parke hill.' However, 140 deer still roamed in the park, and hunting long continued as a favourite pastime. There were 1,200 deer in Sheffield Park in 1637 and 280 deer in Tankersley Park in 1653.

The wealth of the gentry was based primarily upon their agricultural estates, so prudent families were concerned to improve their management and farming methods. Thus, during the reign of Charles I, Christopher Copley enclosed land at Wadworth and planted trees, orchards and hopyards, and the Bosviles redistributed strips and enclosed land at Warmsworth and Thorne. Much depended upon the industry and initiative of individuals. In his family history, Sir John Reresby of Thrybergh attributed the fluctuations in his family's fortunes to the different characters of his ancestors. Thomas Reresby, who died in 1587, was an efficient landlord who added several pieces of property to his estate, but Sir Thomas (1557-1619) was extravagant and his Derbyshire property had to be mortgaged. Sir George (1586-1628) was a 'great manager at home', but he had expensive tastes and his ventures into horse-breeding were financially unsound, so that he was unable to redeem the Derbyshire property. Finally, Sir John (1611-46) was forced to sell land and ran up huge debts through supporting the wrong side in the Civil War.

20   Industry

Iron In the western half of the county many families were fortunate enough to have mineral resources upon their estates. The exploitation of these deposits needed capital, but usually resulted in a steady profit. For instance, the Strelleys of Beauchief were much involved in the lead trade, the Greenes of Thundercliffe Grange mined coal, and the Barnbys, Cutlers, Rockleys and Wortleys had their own ironworks. The 'Wortley group' on the River Don eventually comprised two forges, a wire mill, a slitting mill and a tin-plate mill. A bloomery had been worked here in the Elizabethan period, and 'iron smithies' were referred to in a renewal lease granted by Sir Francis Wortley in 1621. The building of a wire mill in 1624 increased the demand for rod iron, and by 1638 we have clear evidence of two forges. The present top forge dates from 1727 and is being restored in its beautiful rural setting by an enthusiastic band of industrial archaeologists.

Charcoal blast furnaces and water-powered forges had been introduced into Yorkshire and Derbyshire by the 1580s. Attercliffe forge is recorded by name in 1587, and blast furnaces had been established at Kimberworth and Wadsley Bridge by the end of the century. But these new methods did not immediately replace the old, and the medieval practice of smelting iron over a charcoal hearth known as a bloomery and of forging by hand continued well into the seventeenth century. The 'Barnsley Smithies' at Monk Bretton were described in 1589 as 'a pair of smithies or Iron Mills' driven by 'ould smithie wheels', and a lease to two Silkstone yeomen in 1607 referred to 'One Paire of Iron Smithies, Iron Mills, or Iron fforges ... commonly called Silkstone Smythies.' Bloomeries could be large concerns, and the excavation of Rockley Smithies by David Crossley and Denis Ashurst has revealed a dam, three waterwheels for bellows, a bloom-hearth, a string hearth, a reheating hearth and another hearth of unknown purpose, all dating from the period 1500-1640. The site has been obliterated by the M1 motorway, but part of a wheel is preserved at the Abbeydale Industrial Hamlet. Documentary evidence adds to our knowledge of this site, for the will of Roger Rockley of Rockley Hall (1552) referred to ironstone mining in Friartail Wood, to the use of his own timber for charcoal, and to bequests to 'every of my smith's workmen'. In 1652 Lionel Copley erected a charcoal blast furnace nearby in place of the old smithies, and, remarkably, this still stands to the height of fifteen feet. Meanwhile, the Spencers of Cannon Hall had replaced the bloomery at Barnby by a furnace before 1650 and they proceeded to build a new furnace in 1656.

The 1652 blast furnace at Rockley would have been a little higher than at present and would have had a raised platform at the southern end to give access to the top. The hearth has gone, but the four sandstone arches of the base survive intact and the heat-resisting sandstone blocks that form the inner lining were shaped so finely as to resemble firebricks. To operate the furnace, fuel was ignited through the top of the stack. The bottom of the furnace was kept closed, but near the base a nozzle (tuyere) enabled air to be blasted into the furnace by means of a pair of bellows. These were driven by a water wheel whose dams can be traced in outline to the south of the site. The blast caused the rapid combustion of the fuel. Lime was added through the top of the stack so as to reduce the non-combustible compounds such as silica and alumina into a liquid state. The combustible matter escaped through the top as gas, and the slag was tapped off at the base. Ore and fuel were constantly stacked high in the furnace shaft, and when the iron was sufficiently molten it was made to flow into moulds. By this method Rockley furnace was capable of producing nearly 400 tons of pig iron each year, an output that was typical of the charcoal blast furnaces of that era.

The local ironstone was of average quality only and much of the iron produced was sold to the nailers or the wiredrawers. Nail-making was a craft that had flourished since medieval times in the villages immediately to the north of the cutlery district, in and around Ecclesfield, Chapeltown, Hoyland and the surrounding hamlets. At this period the nailers were

61

Rockley blast furnace is a remarkable survival from the charcoal era. Built in 1652 by Lionel Copley, the leading ironmaster in the region, it produced nearly 400 tons of pig iron each year. Recent excavations have revealed the wheel-pit and the casting floor. The furnace is the oldest surviving example in the country, and possibly in Europe.

62

An aerial view of bell pits in the north-western corner of Tankersley park. They were worked by ironstone miners when the medieval hunting park was given over to industry in the late eighteenth century. The bell pit technique was used in the Middle Ages. (Cambridge University Collection, Copyright Reserved).

normally part-time farmers, like most craftsmen up and down the country. The Barnsley wiredrawers had the reputation of manufacturing the best wire in the kingdom during the reign of James I. They made hard wire for the teeth of cotton- and wool-cards and for fish hooks, and softer wire for the needles that were used in later times in the Midlands stocking frames.

Important developments in metalworking took place within and around Hallamshire, for during Queen Elizabeth's reign, George, the sixth Earl of Shrewsbury, was one of the nation's leading industrial entrepreneurs. He had forges at Attercliffe, Goodrich (Herefordshire) and Shifnal (Shropshire), extensive woods for charcoal, seams of ironstone, and mines in Sheffield Park that were producing 1,200 tons of coal per annum in the early 1580s at a yearly profit of £65. In the 1560s he installed an improved blast furnace for the refining and smelting of lead, of the type patented by a German engineer, Christopher Schütz, and William Humfrey, the assay-master of the Mint. Then, during the late 1570s he spent £500 a year on the purchase of lead ore, and by 1585 he was shipping well over 100 tons of lead a year from his warehouse at Bawtry. By that time he was probably smelting more lead than anyone else in the country. He also provided the local cutlers with the high quality steel that was necessary for their finest products by importing Spanish steel through Bawtry. His successor to the earldom did not have the same interest in local industry and it soon became estate policy to lease the plant and minerals to local men. Lionel Copley of the parish of Whiston took full advantage of this opportunity. In 1603 he took a lease of Attercliffe forge, by 1637 he had converted the Sheffield fulling mill into a forge, and in 1641 he erected two furnaces and two forges at Wardsend. He also obtained leases of the Conisbrough ironworks and Rockley furnace, and by the middle of the seventeenth century he was the leading figure in the South Yorkshire iron trade.

Coal Coal was mined on an increasingly large scale during the sixteenth and seventeenth centuries, for it was in demand not only as a domestic fuel, but in the metalworkers' smithies, the manufacture of glass and pottery, and in such crafts as dyeing. The shallow pits for which there is documentary evidence before 1700 lay chiefly at or near the heart of the old coalfield at Abdy, Ardsley, Barnsley, Brampton, Brierley, Cawthorne, Chapeltown, Crookesmoor, Cudworth, Darton, Dodworth, Ecclesall, Gleadless, Greasbrough, Handsworth, Hooton Roberts, Hoyland, Kimberworth, Kiveton, Monk Bretton, Mortomley, Rotherham, Shafton, Sheffield, Silkstone, Staincross, Swinton, Tankersley, Thundercliffe Grange, Thurnscoe, Underbank, Waleswood, Wentworth, Whiston and Worsbrough, though a few lay further east right at the edge of the Magnesian Limestone belt at Barnburgh, Denaby and Hooton Pagnell. There were undoubtedly other mines for which no records have survived. Some of the large landowners were actively engaged in mining their own coal, but others were content to lease their pits to local farmer colliers, such as Robert Hartley of Mortomley, who in 1592 bequeathed land and 'two mynes of Mr. Wortley', which he rented at £13 6s 8d per annum. The Crown also leased its mines, and in 1649 those on Barnsley Moor and Skiers Moor were said to be worth £26 13s 4d and £36 a year, respectively.

Cutlery and Allied Trades Literary references show that Sheffield cutlery had a favourable national reputation during the Elizabethan and Stuart period. Until the Cutlers' Company was incorporated in 1624 the metal workers were organised by the manorial courts of the lordship of Hallamshire. The earliest surviving regulations date from 1565, but these were merely restatements of 'the ancient customs and ordinances' that were necessary to preserve Sheffield's reputation for skill and quality. Manorial control was advantageous to the cutlers as long as the lord took an active interest. Indeed, in 1614 cutlers from the Derbyshire villages of Eckington, Newbold and Whittington opted to work under the lord's supervision. But after the death of Earl Gilbert in 1616 the lords were absentees and the cutlers no longer enjoyed the benefits of protection. In 1621, therefore, they petitioned Parliament for an act of incorporation, and three years later this was granted. The new company obtained jurisdiction over the manufacture of knives, sickles, shears, scissors and other cutlery ware within a six-mile radius of the borders of Hallamshire.

They were joined in 1676 by the awlbladesmiths and in 1682 by the scythesmiths and filesmiths.

About 500 men claimed the right to the freedom of the company on the grounds that they had been occupied in the trade prior to incorporation. Most of these cutlers were those self-employed craftsmen who were to remain the characteristic figures in the trade, but some were also 'able to set on work many poor men . . . who have very small means of maintenance of living other than by their hard and daily labour as workmen.' Away from the town centre, the typical metalworker was a part-time farmer like the majority of rural craftsmen at that time. In 1558, for instance, Robert Wilkinson of Attercliffe bequeathed the lease of a farm as well as the 'biggest harthe with all the gear' and the 'stithe with all the gear that belong to my lytle harthe and a glasier and a vice, also one hollow whele', and in the same year Robert Skergell was described as a Sheffield yeoman, but his bequests included 'smythe gaire' and 'whelle gaire' as well as livestock and corn.

The bulk of the probate inventories made before 1689 in the diocese of York have been destroyed, but those parts of South Yorkshire that once lay in the Derbyshire parishes of Norton and Eckington have inventories which survive from the mid sixteenth century onwards. They provide plenty of evidence of dual occupations in the secondary metal trades. For example, Christopher Barten, a Norton Woodseats nailer who died in 1604, had personal estate valued at £75, which included £28 worth of farmstock, comprising six kine, one calf, two mares and a filly, two swine, and a crop of hardcorn and oats; Robert Gillott of Norton Lees, scythesmith (1628) had farm stock and equipment valued at over £23, as well as 100 rough scythes that he had manufactured in his smithy; and Henry Brownell of Jordanthorpe (1634) had farm goods worth £29, and 256 scythes that were valued at £17 5s 4d.

From 1559 to 1627 the baptism registers of Norton parish normally recorded the occupation of the fathers. Of the ninety three men whose occupations were given in the twenty years following October 1559, thirty-six were craftsmen. They included eleven scythesmiths, one scythe-grinder, one scythe-seller, two nailers, one cutler, one smith, one blacksmith, three iron smelters, five charcoal burners, three carpenters, two woodmen, two tailors, one leather-worker, one weaver, and a slater. Some of the others may also have been involved in the local trades. George Urton of Lightwood was described as yeoman upon his death in 1623, but his probate inventory included 'Iron, Steele and sithes in his stock together with Debtes dewe . . . £80', and William Bullock of Norton, esquire (1667), was a gentleman-manufacturer on a considerable scale, specialising in hoes and axes.

The scythesmith's art consisted in sandwiching a piece of high-quality steel between two pieces of wrought iron, then gripping them in long-handled tongs and placing them in a hearth until they were hot enough to be forged. The forging could be done by hand over an anvil, but as early as 1489 water-power was used to drive tilt hammers for this purpose. The welded iron and steel was then slit lengthways to make two scythes; again, either by hand or by using the same tilt hammer. The scythes were then hardened and tempered and ground at the wheel. The various rivers and streams in the steep-sided valleys of the Hallamshire region were ideal for this purpose. Each waterwheel turned several grindstones, and when John Harrison surveyed Hallamshire in 1637 he observed, 'These Rivers are very profitable unto the Lord in regard to the Mills and Cutler wheeles that are turned by theire streames, which are imployed for the grinding of knives by four or five hundred Master Workmen.'

The act of incorporation of 1624 claimed that the Hallamshire cutlers made 'knives of the best edge, wherewith they serve the most partes of this kingdome and other foreign countries.' Information about markets at this period is difficult to come by, but most of the ware was probably sold by itinerant packmen. When Robert Secker, otherwise known as Clarke of Attercliffe, died at Worcester in the winter of 1580-1, he left three packhorses with a large quantity of knives, and the debts that were owed to him show that he had been selling his goods in Worcestershire, Warwickshire and Herefordshire. But the cutlers' major country markets seem to have been in North-Eastern and Eastern England, and a considerable quantity of ware was sent overland or down the coast to London.

The Blythes of the Bishops' House, Norton Lees, were the outstanding family in the scythe trade. The William Blythe who was responsible for adding the stone wing to the house died in 1632 with personal estate worth £641. His farm stock was valued at £251 and he was leasing the Heeley corn mill and the nearby grinding wheel, as well as renting smithies and equipment to smiths or grinders who were producing scythes for him. His inventory goes on to list no fewer than 1,900 scythes, worth in all £165 10s 0d. These consisted of 650 long scythes, 450 scythes of a second sort, 450 of a third sort, and 350 Scottish scythes. In addition to all this he had 2 tons 11 cwt of iron, worth £38 10s 0d, and steel valued at £8 10s 0d. His trade stock accounted for a total of £231. In 1666 his son and namesake had over 2,000 scythes at the time of his death. His stock included specialist Holderness and Scottish scythes and he had trade connections in Beverley, Boroughbridge, Morpeth, Newcastle, Wakefield and York. The manufacture of scythes was obviously already a sophisticated business.

Textiles Numerous sixteenth and seventeenth-century wills show that the manufacture of cloth was still widespread in South Yorkshire. In the east, clothiers were able to take advantage of the major wool market that was held at Doncaster. Thus, the corporation accounts of 1667 record the rent paid by Richard Speight, dyer, for his tenters, and a lease of 1629 refers to fifteen drapers' stalls and one wool shop in the market place. The weavers, walkers and shearmen of Doncaster were organized into a guild, and so were the tailors. Sprotbrough had a fulling mill in the seventeenth century, and to this day there is a Tenter Lane in Warmsworth and a Tenter Balk Lane in Adwick le Street. Undyed kerseys were the major products, but coarse cloths known as 'penistones', 'northern penistones' or 'penistone dozens' were manufactured in parts of the West Riding and Lancashire and sold as far afield as London. They presumably took their name from the moorland parish in the west. Penistones were normally sold by Wakefield merchants, but as late as 1640 the men of Barnsley were still stubbornly preserving their cloth market. The craft of linen weaving also flourished as a by-employment in parts of the county, though Christopher Crofts of Whitley was rather unusual in being described in 1629 as a specialist linen webster. Both trades were intimately associated with agriculture, and they helped to provide work for all the members of a household. A typical figure was William Rodes of Sheffield Park, who in 1556 bequeathed four cows as well as two linen looms, a woollen loom, 'a carsay geare and a playn geare'. Some did very well out of the trade, and the Elmhirsts of Houndhill rose to gentry status through their investment in sheep-farming and the manufacture of cloth.

In the eastern and central parts of the county, men, women and children earned extra income by the hand-knitting of tough, hard-wearing woollen stockings. There were reputedly 120 knitters in and around Doncaster in 1595, and a lawsuit from the reign of Charles I reveals that two merchants from Doncaster and Rotherham were exporting woollen stockings and hose to London. At the close of the seventeenth century, Dorothy Wells, a Doncaster widow, had in her chambers linen worth £8 5s 0d, wool and oil worth £2 8s 0d, and five knitted petticoats, twenty knitted waistcoats, fifteen pairs of knitted drawers, nine dozen and eight caps and socks, and 23 pair of hose valued at £21 2s 9d. Half a century later Emanuel Bowen could write that Doncaster still 'has a goode Trade for Stockings and knit Waist Coats', but soon afterwards the trade dwindled rapidly because of competition from the framework knitters of the Midlands. It survived much longer in the Yorkshire Dales.

Tanning During this period South Yorkshire was also a noted tanning centre. The industry flourished in the first place because it was able to draw upon a ready supply of local hides from the predominantly cattle-rearing foothills in the west and the lowlands in the east. Thus, a tanyard was recorded at Thorne in 1483, and at Doncaster the corporation leased tanneries to local men in Fishergate. In the west, William Rawson of the parish of Sheffield was described as a tanner upon his death in 1550, and by 1637 his descendants had tanyards at Norwood and Upperthorpe and were soon to acquire one at Wardsend. Harrison's survey of 1637 also mentions three other tanners in the Ponds and William Wood's 'Tan house of 3 bayes in the Tanyard' at Wardsend. Tanners also worked in the surrounding villages, and by the early seventeenth century the South Yorkshire tanning industry had grown to such an extent that a great number of extra hides had to be imported from London, via Hull and Bawtry. The inventory of John Brook of Dodworth, for example, refers in 1649 to 'Money return'd to London for buying Hides, £20.' The history of this industry has been rather neglected, but it was obviously of major importance in the national economy.

21 Farming

The western parts   These industries added greatly to the wealth of the area and helped many a family to earn a moderate living. Nevertheless, they were subsidiary to farming as the basic means of livelihood. The annual rhythm of the farming year still provided a sense of order and continuity, for even the townsmen were not far away from the fields and were dependent upon the markets. The paines or by-laws issued by the court of the manors of Greasbrough and Barbot Hall in 1574 illustrate the way in which agricultural activities were still organised around the old religious calendar. Swine had to be ringed before the feast of St Bartholomew and kept that way until the feast of the Purification of the Blessed Virgin Mary; they then had to be kept yoked from Candlemas until the harvest was gathered. Everyone had to fence his strips in the winter corn field within nine days after Michaelmas and the spring corn field had to be fenced by the first of March. The regulations were designed to ensure fairness for all and an orderly arrangement of communal farming. People were forbidden to plough the headlands and balks of the common fields, to graze their cattle in the common meadows, to take hedge timber for firewood, to fell holly trees (for their leaves were valuable as winter feed for sheep and cattle), or to put 'corrupt cattell or scabbed horses' on the common pastures. A similar set of regulations issued by the manorial court at Ecclesfield survives for the year 1608. In addition to the usual laws, the jury ordered that mastiffs must always be muzzled, that clothes must not be washed or horses allowed to drink at the common wells, and that ditches must be scoured. The jurors of the manorial courts were the ordinary tenant farmers of the manor and their rules were designed to enhance the well-being of the community.

   The probate inventory of John Bingley of Bolton upon Dearne, drawn up on 8 November 1632, gives a good indication of the livestock, crops and equipment of a farmer living and working on the Coal-Measure sandstones. At the time of his death Bingley had eight oxen, five horses, three milk cows, one heifer and a flock of sheep, worth in all £52 6s 8d, wheat, barley, oats, peas and rye unthreshed in his barn, worth £59 6s 8d, hay valued at £15, eighteen acres of winter wheat already sown and five acres prepared for barley, valued at £60, four small waggons described as iron-bound wains, three ploughs, five harrows, fences, standhecks containing hay for cows, troughs, yokes, harness and other gear, and timber for making other items, together worth a further £14 8s 2d.

Bingley and most of his neighbours kept a balance between animals and crops, but further west the emphasis was on rearing cattle and sheep and on dairying. A letter from Sir Edward Stanhope of Edlington to the justices of the peace in 1592, in which he complained that the inhabitants of Barnby Dun had blocked the passage of the River Don by placing stepping-stones there for themselves and their sheep, stated that the people of Barnsley and the villages further west were dependent upon this route for their supply of corn from Lincolnshire and the eastern parts of Yorkshire. The pastoral way of life in the west allowed families sufficient time to pursue a craft, and the fact that only light payments were demanded by manorial custom enabled people to save the small amount of capital that was necessary for industrial investment. The farms were small, but a dual occupation and extensive common rights helped to provide a satisfactory living. The records of the taxes known as the lay subsidies of the 1540s show that large numbers of people each paid a small amount, both in Hallamshire and in the townships of Barnsley, Brierley, Cudworth and Thurgoland. Customs varied greatly from one manor to another, but most of the tenants in the western parts of the county seem to have had terms that were favourable to them.

The land at the edge of the wastes had now been cleared back to the limits of cultivation that had been reached before the fourteenth-century decay of the economy, and the best common pastures were already stinted or even enclosed. The use of Rotherham common, for example, was restricted by 1638, and a letter written to Sir Thomas Wentworth in 1630 shows that the Wortleys were not the only lords to enclose land against their tenants' wishes, for Sir Francis Foljambe was said to have taken in three-quarters of the common between Rawmarsh and Kilnhurst and to have threatened to ruin his opponents with the cost of going to law, 'sayinge hee will pave it with silver before he will losse it.' Many of the common fields were enclosed quietly and peacefully with the agreement of all; a deed of 1642, for instance, refers to 'One Close or parcell of arrable land lately enclosed out of the Comon ffeilde in Worsbrough . . . called Midlefield', and though Shafton was still farmed on an open-field system in 1597, only a few parcels of strips remained unenclosed a hundred years later. On the other hand much remained to be reallotted at the time of parliamentary enclosure, and many places continued to work the old system. Thus in 1649 Barnsley still had four common arable fields, with unstinted grazing on the common pasture and the right for all the freeholders and tenants to put their animals into the common fields after harvest.

The limestone area The most fertile part of South Yorkshire was still the Magnesian Limestone belt. When Henry VIII visited the county in 1541 Bishop Tunstall escorted him to Scawsby Lees to see 'one of the greatest and richest valleys that ever [the bishop] had found in all his travels thro' Europe.' Similarly, in 1632 the lord's lands in Loversall were said to be 'of great tillage'. The small, compact villages of this region were normally under the dominion of powerful squires, such as the Annes of Frickley and Burghwallis, the Jacksons of Hickleton, and the Osbornes of Kiveton and Thorpe Salvin. This part of the county contained many deserted settlements and several communities that continued to shrink during the sixteenth and seventeenth centuries as poor prices for corn and wool, combined with high labour costs, drove many middling farmers into poverty. A survey of the parish of Hooton Pagnell shows that in 1548 the lord and his eleven tenants farmed a third of the cultivated land and the remaining two-thirds was owned by nineteen freeholders; by 1763 the lord had acquired all but thirteen acres of glebe and the 70 acres of land that was divided between the three surviving freeholders.

A great deal of painstaking research still needs to be done in order to date and explain this process. In most cases the depopulation of a village was not an abrupt event but was the result of gradual decay. Wildthorpe, for instance, had been weakened seriously during the medieval period, but it still had its three open-fields in the seventeenth century. At Owston almost fifty freeholders owned land in 1343 and ninety people paid the poll tax in 1379, including twelve who were rich enough to be assessed at more than the basic rate. However, in 1545 the community was dominated by William Adam, who was taxed on goods worth £12, and who farmed the Duchy of Lancaster lands, together with another 184 acres and the pasture rights in the park. Today Owston is little more than a hamlet under the shadow of the hall.

In the north-eastern corner of the parish of Tickhill a solitary farmstead marks the site of the former village of Stancil. This was an ancient settlement, for the place-name (which means 'the stone dwelling hall') presumably refers to the Roman villa that has been discovered 200 yards or so away from the farm. Stancil was recorded in Domesday Book, and in 1379 fifteen married couples and twenty-seven single persons were old enough to be assessed for the poll tax. Four heads of households were farmer-craftsmen who were taxed at more than the basic rate. Yet two centuries later Stancil was farmed by only four families, and soon the settlement was reduced to the status of a single farm. Probably it had already begun to decay by the 1520s or 1530s, when John Wirral, a Doncaster merchant, bought the manors of both Stancil and Loversall.

There are signs that Loversall, too, has shrunk, for the church is now almost isolated from the rest of the village, and tell-tale mounds speak of former buildings near the churchyard.

The poor corn prices that ruined so many small farmers persuaded those who survived to turn over much of this fine arable land to pasture. This could be done under an open-field system by agreements to convert certain strips into grass leys or by enclosing whole blocks of furlongs. At Hooton Pagnell, for instance, the 937 acres of open fields in 1595 had been reduced by partial enclosure to 553 acres by 1754. Evidence of such agreements is hard to come by, but enclosure must be seen as a continuous process that started in the sixteenth century and which was completed by private acts of parliament in the late eighteenth or early nineteenth centuries. Several villages were enclosed completely long before the age of parliamentary enclosure and no awards survive for the open fields (as distinct from the commons and wastes) of Hickleton, High Melton, Loversall, Marr, South Anston and Thorpe Salvin. In many villages it was also found necessary at an early period to restrict the grazing rights on the commons; at Hooton Pagnell the commons had been stinted since 1570 at least, and a 1652 survey shows that although grazing on Braithwell Moor was unrestricted, the pastures in the nearby Birkwood and Austwood were stinted; that is, the number of animals allowed was in proportion to the size of the farm.

The lowlands In the lowlands to the east pressure on the commons was equally as evident. In 1659, for example, the inhabitants of Austerfield and Misson were in dispute over the grazing rights in a common pasture that had been drained about twelve years previously. The people of these lowlands followed a pastoral way of life. Few of the farms were large, and a multitude of smallholdings had been created as a result of a system of inheritance, whereby all sons received a share of the property. A sufficient livelihood could be obtained only because of generous rights of pasture and turbary and because of opportunities for by-employments involving the manufacture of linen and the digging of turf. Much of the lowlands lay under water for most of the year but in dry summers they provided rich grazing. Some attempts at partial drainage had been made during the medieval period, but vast tracts of land were still flooded regularly.

A commission of several South Yorkshire landowners which had been set up during the reign of James I had inquired into the possibility of a massive drainage scheme, but they had decided that such a project was impracticable. However, in 1626 the financial difficulties of Charles I caused the royal advisers to reconsider the scheme and to send for Cornelius Vermuyden, the Dutch engineer. The project was financed by Dutch and Flemish families for whom Vermuyden acted as agent. It was agreed that a third of the drained land should be granted to Vermuyden and his company, a third should compensate the local inhabitants for the loss of their common rights, and a third should remain with the king in lieu of his manorial and hunting rights within Hatfield Chase. The king's share was bought later by Vermuyden. This was one of the first of the great drainage schemes of the seventeenth century. A vast area of approximately 70,000 acres, extending into Lincolnshire, was to be drained, and a great number of Flemish workers were brought over to work on the project.

The periodic flooding of Hatfield Chase was caused by the overflowing of the rivers Don, Torne, Idle, Aire and Went and of smaller streams such as the Bycarrsdyke as they made their way towards the Humber. It was difficult to move the waters, as in some parts the land was only four feet above sea level. In the chase, the River Don formed two branches, and Vermuyden soon came to the conclusion that the sluggish meanderings of the southern branch were the chief problem. He resolved to divert the water into the straight channel, now known as the Dutch river, which had been cut from the northern branch of the Don at some unknown date prior to the map of Inclesmoor, which had been engraved in the early fifteenth century. Vermuyden's scheme involved the digging of a multitude of small drains, a surprising number of which still fulfil their original function. The southern branch of the Don eventually became redundant, but it can still be traced in part near the county boundary.

In 1627 Vermuyden announced that the project had been completed, but his claim was disputed hotly. Land in the Sykehouse and Fishlake area that had not been flooded previously had been put in danger by the project. A letter from Richard Bridges of Sykehouse, addressed to Sir Thomas Wentworth on 6 September 1630, gives a graphic account of the damage that was done. He wrote as 'a woefull spectator of the Lamentable destruction of my native soyle & countrie', who had seen crops destroyed,

63

In 1626 Cornelius Vermuyden closed the southern branch of the River Don and diverted all the water into the northern channel, which is still known as the Dutch River. The fields beyond were created as a result of Vermuyden's drainage.

houses damaged and families in pitiful distress. 'Thus have strangers prevayled to destroy our Inheritance', he wrote. In other parts of the chase the farmers claimed that annual flooding was beneficial to their pastures and that their new allotments were insufficient compensation for the loss of their common rights. Riots broke out in which tools were burnt, embankments were destroyed, and the Flemings were assaulted. At the height of the violence some of the foreigners were killed.

Faced with this hostility many Dutch and Flemish families returned home. Most of the settlers were not the financiers of the scheme but merely their tenants. However, despite the troubles, a colony was established east of Thorne and Hatfield Woodhouse in the newly-drained area that became known as the Levels. In Fishlake and Sykehouse passions subsided once steps were taken to prevent further flooding. Beyond the Levels farming continued upon much the same pattern as before, for there had been no attempt to drain the whole area; a great deal of land remained subject to regular flooding until the nineteenth century, when steam engines were employed to pump the water away. Nevertheless, the scheme had a great effect on the area. It led to the complete decline of Tudworth (a small settlement on the redundant branch of the Don) and it was responsible for the growth of Goole as a port at the eastern end of the Dutch River. Thorne also benefited as an inland port, and during the brief protectorate of Richard Cromwell (1658-60) its inhabitants obtained a licence for a weekly market and an annual fair. Thorne soon became one of the busiest little towns in South Yorkshire.

22 Markets

The most important market centre in South Yorkshire was still that at Doncaster. Already there was pressure on the available space in the ancient market place, and in 1605 the corporation agreed 'that the horse fair be held in Hallgate from the Pynfould to the Hall Crosse; that the beast fair be held in the market place; the sheep fair between the Butchers Cross and the Pynfould in Hallgate; and the swine fair in Sepulchre Gate within the bars.' Then in 1612 a more permanent site was found for the Horse Fair, when it was moved to Waterdale at the southern edge of the town. The triangular shape of the fair ground is still evident despite the busy road that cuts through it. Meanwhile, the wool market had become one of the largest in the kingdom, and sometimes as many as 6,000 fleeces were sold here each Saturday during the summer. A Chancery case during the reign of Charles I shows that buyers came from Derbyshire, Leicestershire, Lincolnshire, Norfolk, Nottinghamshire, Warwickshire and Yorkshire. The corn market was held around the wheat cross, meat and fish were sold in the shambles, poultry were sold on Goose Hill, and by this period permanent shops had been erected in or alongside the former churchyard of St Mary Magdalene, at the heart of the market place. They were separated by narrow little lanes, with names such as Shoe Lane, Meal Lane and Roper Row to describe their various specialisations. The Butchers' Cross stood outside the market place at the junction of High Street and Baxter Gate.

Rotherham was also a successful market centre, with a great beast fair, and Bawtry had now recovered from its period of depression. At the beginning of the seventeenth century it had two wharves for exporting lead, millstones, cutlery and other metalware, and two annual fairs and a weekly market. Barnsley, too, was flourishing, and amongst its marts was a specialised malt fair. Meanwhile, Sheffield's market was no longer able to cope fully with the demands placed upon it. The parish registers reveal a constant surplus of baptisms over burials during the decades between 1561 and 1630, and in 1608 the town was said to consist of 'handicraftes men, in great numbers, who have no means to make their provision but only in the markett, and that the cuntrie there aboutes affoardeth not sufficient stoare of white meates, cheifly butter, and cheese, to serve that towne.' The remedy was to allow Elizabeth Heywood, a local widow, to buy butter and cheese from Ashbourne and other markets for re-sale at Sheffield.

23 The Great Rebuilding

Materials The physical appearance of English towns and villages underwent considerable change during this century. The age of Queen Elizabeth and the Stuart kings was a transitional period during which the use of timber was gradually abandoned in favour of stone or brick. Oak became too scarce and expensive to use on the old lavish scale. In 1649 the parliamentary surveyors reported that at Barnsley there was 'noe wood within the mannor worth the valueing', but that there were 'Quarries of stone and slate in and uppon the wast or common.' By the end of the seventeenth century local stone had ousted timber as the basic building material of the western half of South Yorkshire, and when Celia Fiennes travelled between Hemsworth and Rotherham in 1697 she was struck by the number of fine houses and walls newly built of freestone. Further east, on the Magnesian Limestone, the rebuilding was eventually so complete that very little timber-framing now survives.

At the same time, stone slates, or 'thackstones', were beginning to replace thatch on all but the humblest dwellings. In 1611 William Fenton of Wadsley had a dwelling house, a parlour, and a barn 'all covered with straw in great decay', but a survey taken five years later shows that new buildings in and near Sheffield were all being roofed with slate. Philip Asburrie of Owlerton, for instance, rented '1 dwelling house and Kitchin 3 baies and an outshutt thatcht saveing the Kitchin [which] is nue and slated [and] an old barn of 3 baies thatcht,' and George Oxspring of Sheffield had 'A Thatcht house of 3 baies butting west on the street...alsoe a new dwelling house slated of a bay and an halfe, A Stable 1 bay, and an outshutt thatcht, a barn 2 baies slated.' In 1616 Richard Archdale of the Brushes had merely a 'Dwelling house and mistall [cowshed] of 2 Baies Thatcht', but a note was added in 1672 to say, 'now 7 Bay all slated',

In the eastern part of South Yorkshire the few timber-framed buildings that survive are nearly all faced with brick. Buildings at Austerfield and Stainforth still have their corner posts visible, but the gable of a house in Tickhill, which was exposed when its neighbour was demolished, shows how easily an ancient frame could be disguised behind an ordinary-looking exterior. References to Brickhill Carr and Tylehouse Kilne in a 1607 survey of Hatfield show that bricks were being made locally by the beginning of the seventeenth century, but the earliest surviving brick house that can be dated is one that was built near Sykehouse in 1702. During the late 1690s Abraham de la Pryme wrote in his unpublished history of the village of Hatfield.

The manner of the building that it formerly had were all of wood, clay, and plaster, but now that way of building is quite left of, for every one now, from the richest to the poorest, will not build except with bricks: so that now from about 80 years ago (at which time bricks was first seen, used, and made in this parish), they have been wholly used, and now there scarce is one house in the town that dos not, if not wholy, yet for the most part, consist of that lasting and genteel sort of building; many of which are also built according to the late model with cut brick and covered over with Holland tyle, which gives a brisk and pleasant air to the town, and tho' many of the houses be little and despicable without, yet they are neat, well furnished, and most of them ceiled with the whitest plaster within.

The gypsum plaster was 'digged up in great Quantity and plenty' nearby in the Isle of Axholme. A few undated examples of these houses still survive in Hatfield.

Halls Many of the characteristics of the larger medieval houses were shared by their Elizabethan and Jacobean successors, such as those at Houndhill and (just north of the county boundary) at Wheatley Hill. These houses are distinctive in style and are unlike those of, say, East Anglia, the Weald, or the West Midlands. Large panels with herringbone designs covering entire storeys catch the eye immediately, and interest is held by the closely-set diagonal studs in the upper gables. Sometimes, as at Houndhill, these studs are parallel to the rafters; at other times, as at Wheatley Hill, they are arranged at right angles to them; and at the Bishops' House at Norton Lees the pattern is different from one gable to the other. The ground plans of these houses, however, are similar to those found all over the country. The substantial yeomen and minor gentry of Elizabethan and early-Stuart times built houses which were essentially in the medieval tradition with a central hall and two cross-wings, one of

The Elmhirst family still live in this fine Elizabethan or early-Stuart house built by their ancestors at Houndhill, in the parish of Worsbrough. The Elmhirsts prospered as sheep-farmers and clothiers and were soon able to add a stone wing to the earlier timber-framed building.

which was sometimes separated from the hall by an 'entry' or cross-passage. This plan is illustrated by the parliamentary surveyors' description of the (demolished) Barnsley Hall. In 1649 this building was 'an ancient strong timber house...consisting of a spacious Hall, two parlours, two other nether rooms with a buttery 3 lodgeing Chambers, all which rooms are at the South end of the house from the entry, alsoe a kitchin a parlour a dairy house with 2 Chambers over them at the north end of the house from the entry.'

It was not unusual during the transitional period from timber to stone for men like the Elmhirsts of Houndhill to build one wing with oak and a later wing with sandstone. (The arrangement of the roofing timbers at Houndhill shows that the stone wing was added later.) During the seventeenth century the use of timber frames was gradually abandoned. Houses such as the Old Hall at Brampton en le Morthen, Housley Hall at Chapeltown, or the Micklethwaites' house at Ingbirchworth were of the same proportions as earlier halls, but they were built of stone. Furthermore, the timber-framed houses that were extended or altered during this period were restyled by the masons, and in some cases their ancient plan was altered beyond recognition.

The characteristic seventeenth-century halls of South Yorkshire were built entirely of local stone. The great landowners and some of the gentry had already begun to build in this way during the Elizabethan period. In the 1570s the Earl of Shrewsbury built the three-storeyed Turret House, which stands intact at the Sheffield Manor Lodge, and it must have been about this time that the Saviles erected the hall, which is now a picturesque ruin in the park at Tankersley. Henry Sandford had also completed his splendid manor house on the Magnesian Limestone at Thorpe Salvin before his death in 1582. The design was apparently influenced by the (demolished) Elizabethan hall at Chatsworth, obtaining its effect by its

The crumbling facade of Thorpe Salvin hall. This important Elizabethan building was erected by Henry Sandford and was apparently modelled upon the (demolished) Elizabethan hall at Chatsworth. The building was abandoned when the owners built a new house in Kiveton park at the end of the seventeenth century.

height and symmetry and by the round corner turrets and the dramatic chimney stacks that pierced the skyline. Only the crumbling south facade and the step-gabled gateway survive, but the building was evidently rectangular in plan and perhaps arranged around a small courtyard. The larger windows are on the top floor, which suggests that the architect followed the Chatsworth plan with a skied gallery and a great chamber.

Part of a building which was erected in 1584 is incorporated in the present Whitley Hall. It was built by William Parker, whose family had long been landowners and scythemakers in the parish of Norton. The dam that powered their scythe-grinding wheel at Whitley now serves as an ornamental pool. A few seventeenth-century halls have date-stones. Fulwood Hall was erected in 1620, part of Totley in 1623, Cat Hill in 1634 and Bullhouse in 1655. Undated halls, such as those at Laughton, Nabbs, Onesacre, Worsbrough and Water Hall, Penistone, obviously belong to the same tradition, as did demolished examples at Barnburgh, Darnall, Great Houghton, Greenhill, Kimberworth, Wigtwizzle and elsewhere. Their plain and sombre style allows them to blend perfectly into the landscape, but at the same time varied ground plans and the use of fanciful detail give each house an individual appearance. The doorways and gables, in particular, provided opportunities for enterprise, and small rose-windows relieve the symmetry of the mullions, while, internally, plaster-ceilings and fireplaces such as the one built in 1623 for Stephen Bright of Carbrook, or the panelling still *in situ* at Houndhill, allowed scope for display and imagination. Thus, Cat Hill Hall is built in the regional style, three storeys high, with dormer gables and mullioned and transomed windows, but it achieves a marked individuality with its projecting central porch, the unusually high-pitched gables, and a small cusped window in one of the upper storeys. Only the demolished hall at Wigtwizzle had a similar three-storeyed central porch instead of the usual symmetrical or recessed front.

The ashlar masonry of Bullhouse Hall has recently been restored to its original appearance, free at last of the soot deposited by passing trains. The building has many of the architectural details of Cat Hill but its design is very different. There is no central porch, and the doorway has been reduced to a minor feature, so that first impressions are of the odd row of gables with their curious finials and of the range of mullioned windows. The symmetry of the front is broken by a large projecting wing with a gable of a pitch flatter than the other three. Inside, the original panelling is preserved and there is a possibility that part of an older house is incorporated in the building. The Rich family were country gentlemen who came to Bullhouse in the fifteenth century. The present hall was built by Sylvanus Rich in 1655, and extended in 1688 by his son, Elkanah, who also built the independent chapel just beyond the hall in 1692.

Smaller houses Much improvement also took place at a lower social level during 'The Age of the Great Rebuilding'. All over the country farmers and craftsmen were becoming more prosperous and were using their profits to improve their accommodation. From the earliest years of the reign of Elizabeth the wills of local yeomen and husbandmen refer to a

66

Bullhouse hall was built by Sylvanus Rich in 1655 and enlarged by his son, Elkanah, in 1688. The Riches were Puritan gentlemen and prominent figures in the parish of Penistone. In 1692 they erected an Independent chapel in their own grounds.

whole series of minor refinements, as extra rooms were added and new furniture was acquired. Thus, the 'iron chimneys' that replaced the old open hearths are named as bequests in the wills of Thomas Hinchcliffe of Carlton, near Royston (1558), of John Smythe of Worsbrough (1561), and of many others about that time, and in 1584 Robert Howle proudly bequeathed 'all the glass in the windows in all places in and about my new dwelling house at Attercliffe.'

Most of the smaller Elizabethan and Stuart houses were replaced during later rebuildings in the eighteenth and nineteenth centuries, but the limited evidence that remains suggests that they were comparable in size and arrangements with those found elsewhere in the country. Their ground plan was simple and essentially medieval, with a range of three rooms and an off-centre 'entry' between two of the rooms. However, they were superior to older houses in having upstairs rooms, or chambers, and a chimney stack instead of an open hearth and an air vent. A house in the village street at Braithwell still has its original wooden-framed chimney. In the eastern half of the county, all the surviving examples have their chimney stacks inserted in the passage behind the door so as to heat the rooms at both sides in the fashion of southern and eastern England. The fashion of the Highland zone is illustrated by a house at Dore, which was built in 1686 and later converted into cottages. Here, the chimney stack is to the left of the original entrance, so that only the main living room was heated. Houses in either of these styles rarely have date-stones. Good examples are Home Farm at Hooton Pagnell and Ashton House at Braithwell, which have the chamfered mullioned windows and drip-moulds that were typical of the Elizabethan and early-Stuart period. Others are sometimes heavily disguised with pebble-dash coatings, blocked doors and windows, and later extensions, and naturally there was considerable variation upon the basic plan, for houses were built to suit individual taste. A number of two-room houses with similar chimney arrangements also survive, and quite large houses like Scawsby Hall and a building of 1701 in Northgate, Tickhill, were erected upon this plan. Window styles and other decorative features show that both the two-room and the three-room type continued into the eighteenth century, but the concept is Elizabethan or early-Stuart in origin.

Many poor families, of course, still lived in the most miserable conditions. A survey of Cawthorne in 1638 records twenty families of squatters, who, 'being very poore people and standinge need of releefe have within the compasse of fifty years last past erected poor cottages uppon the wasts within the said Mannors', and the parliamentary survey of Barnsley, taken eleven years later, refers to 'All that ruinous Cottage or barne... called the laythes divided into 4 habitations, wherein 4 familyes of very poore people inhabite.' Similarly, in 1694 a house in Brampton en le Morthen was described as a 'small cottage containing one bay of building

67

Home Farm, Hooton Pagnell, is built to the standard design of many a late-sixteenth or seventeenth-century yeoman's farmhouse. Like many farmhouses in crowded villages, its gable end faces the street.

in great decay.' In the urban centres many families were desperately poor. Of the 66 houses recorded in the 1611 and 1616 surveys of parts of the Sheffield district, twelve had only one bay and perhaps a lean-to, and Nicholas Shooter, who lived in '1 small Cottage 1 Bay thatcht', was typical of several humble people who were gathered in the Water Lane – Castle Green district. A further 23 families had cottages of only two bays (sometimes with outshutts), but there were also nineteen houses with three bays, nine with four bays, and three with as many as five bays.

The humble standard of living of a Conisbrough labourer is evident from the inventory taken upon the death of George Nicholson in September 1651. He was living in a one-storeyed house that consisted of two rooms and a small unheated 'kitchen':

His purse and Apparel, 10s 0d.

Goods in the house: 1 Langsetle, 2s 0d, 1 brasse pott, 3s 4d, 1 spitt and a paire of Tongs, 8d, 2 Pewter dishes, 2s 0d, 1 backstoole 2 Quossions [cushions] with other Uttensils, 1s 8d

Goods in the Parlor: 2 Chists 1 old Cubbard 1 old Chaire a little forme with an old tubb, 3s 4d, 2 stocks & a bench, 1s 0d.

Corne reaped: 3 quarters of Barley, £3, 3 loads of wheat, £2, 2 loads of Peas, 10s 0d, 1 quarter & 5 metts of oats, 16s 0d, 1 Lame cow a heffer & a Calfe, £3 10s 0d, 1 Meare and a ffoale, £5.

Goods in the Kitchin: 2 Little panns and a litle board, 2s 0d, 1 Old bedstead with other imploments, 2s 6d, 4 henns and a Cocke, 2s 6d.

His goods were valued collectively at £16 6s 4d (though the valuations add up to £16 7s 0d), his funeral expenses came to 10s 0d, and he owed seven sums, which amount to £24. He must have been typical of many others of labouring rank.

Smithies A large number of farmhouses in South-West Yorkshire were distinctive in having smithies amongst their outbuildings, for the running of a farm or smallholding was effectively combined with the manufacture of metalware. Few buildings now survive to illustrate the way of life of these farmer-craftsmen. The best example is the Challoner family's smallholding and fork-making complex at Hatfield House Lane, Sheffield. The farmhouse is timber-framed in the style of the sixteenth or seventeenth century. A one-bay structure with thick timbers, which is attached to the north side of the house, was originally open to the roof. It may have served either as a kitchen or as a workshop. A one-bay fork smithy, built of stone, stands detached from and immediately in front of it, and another smithy that once stood nearby has recently been demolished. Across the yard stands a barn of three bays, two of which are supported by crucks; and at right-angles to, and separate from, this barn is a long building, formerly used for stabling, that has the remains of a timber frame in one gable end.

There is plenty of documentary evidence for this way of life during the seventeenth century. For instance, John Harrison's survey of Hallamshire in 1637 records seventeen farms or smallholdings that had smithies attached to them. The following selection from the northern parts of the parish of Ecclesfield illustrates the ways in which the buildings were arranged. Nicholas Carr, a farmer of 78 acres, leased 'a Tenement called Hunter House with a dwelling house of 2 bayes, a heyhouse of 2 bayes a Barne of 3 bayes, an ox house and a stable of 4 bayes a Smithy and a waine house'. His neighbour, William Bower of Cross House, farmed 49 acres and had 'a dwelling house of 3 bayes 2 barns of 3 bayes [and] a Smithy', and Ralph and Henry Smith shared 18½ acres at Cinder Hill, with 'a dwelling house and a Mault House of 6 Bayes a Barne of 5 bayes a Smithey [and] a Cowhouse'. In the hamlet of Potter Hill, Thomas Greene farmed 80 acres, with 'a dwelling house of 4 bayes, a stable and a beast house of 2 bayes, a barne of 3 bayes, another barne of 3 bayes, a Smithy and a wayne house', and nearby, at High Green, Ralph Stones had an 84 acre farm, with 'a dwelling house of 3 bayes, an outhouse of 4 bayes a Smithy of 2 bayes and one baye and an halfe of a Barne.' Several other examples could be quoted from this and earlier surveys. There were also poor craftsmen like James Foster of Ecclesfield Common, who had less than one acre of land with his 'dwelling house and a Smithey of three Bayes a Beast house and a Backside', or William Crosley, who held four acres at Mortomley Lane End, with 'a Dwelling House of 2 bayes a Smithey [and] an Hey house', but the evidence of wills and probate inventories confirms that many of the peasant-craftsmen were men of moderately comfortable means.

24 The Poor

The Elizabethan Poor Laws of 1598 and 1601 placed the responsibility for the poor on 'the Churchwardens of every parish and four substantial householders there . . ., who shall be nominated yearly in Easter week under the hand and seal of two or more Justices of the Peace . . . [and who] shall be called overseers of the poor.' They had the power to levy taxes, to set the poor to work, to establish workhouses, apprentice poor children, and to give relief in the form of clothes, fuel, food and the payment of house-rents to the 'lame, impotent, old, blind, and such other among them being poor and not able to work.' Begging was forbidden and was punishable by whipping.

Prior to these acts the poor were provided for by a mixture of private and public charity. Much of the relief was in the form of occasional doles, notably those distributed at funerals. Endowments of money or land for charitable purposes were rare before the Reformation, and the only recorded instance in South Yorkshire concerns John Moulston of Bradfield, who in 1483 granted the rents of a building and twelve acres of land to the relief of the poor and the maintenance of the church and towards expenditure on various items of local government. After the Reformation men of substance came to feel that it was a religious and social obligation for them to make an endowment. In 1587, for example, George, Earl of Shrewsbury bequeathed £200 to the poor craftsmen of Sheffield and donated further sums to the poor of Rotherham and Chesterfield. Local men who had made their fortunes in London frequently remembered their place of origin when they made their will. Thus, in 1645, Edward Rennick, a merchant-tailor, left £100 to the poor of Doncaster, and in 1632 John Rayney not only provided for the poor of Worsbrough, but established a lectureship for a preacher there and placed the finances of the grammar school upon a sounder footing.

Other men founded almshouses, or 'hospitals.' Such a building was erected in Doncaster in 1562 by Thomas Ellis, a local merchant and alderman. The Shrewsbury almshouses in Sheffield were endowed in 1618 by Gilbert, the seventh earl, but because of a dispute over his will they were not built until 1673; the present buildings date from 1827. Meanwhile, in the parish of Ecclesfield, Sir Richard Scott of Barnes Hall founded an almshouse for six poor people at Barnes Green, which was built in 1639 and demolished in 1962. The best surviving almshouse is undoubtedly the one opposite the church at Arksey, built in 1660 by Sir Bryan Cooke, the son of a Doncaster merchant. The buildings form three sides of a quadrangle, with a high wall along the street and an impressive gateway with an inscription and the Cooke arms. They have, unfortunately, been coated with pebble-dash and re-roofed, but together with the church and the school which Cooke built in 1683, they still form what Pevsner has called 'a delectable oasis'.

The semi-official bodies that catered for the poor obtained their revenue from lands that had once belonged to chantries, guilds and other institutions which had been abolished at the time of the Reformation. The Rotherham feoffees did not receive a formal charter until 1589, but they had been in existence for several years previously. At Ecclesfield, in 1549, fourteen feoffees (or trustees) were appointed to administer the 65½ acres of the former chantry of St Mary for the benefit of the poor, the maintenance of the church and the improvement of the highways. And at Sheffield in 1554, two new bodies were created from the old Burgery: twelve Capital Burgesses were given responsibility for the upkeep of the church, and thirteen Town Trustees provided for the poor and for the highways, administered petty justice, and supervised the archery practice at the Wicker butts. Each of these charitable bodies is still in existence. Doncaster, however, had no need for such an institution, for the corporation had sufficient powers to deal with these matters.

In 1638 the Ecclesfield feoffees built an almshouse, with the aid of a public subscription. The Town Trustees of Sheffield had erected a similar building at West Bar ten years earlier. By 1638 this was operating as a workhouse, for the accounts note the 'charges of the 2 men that cam from Wakefield to have sett children on woorke', and those for 1640 say, 'deliverd further in stock to the woorkehouse, £10'. References to heckles and swingle trees in 1655 show that the work involved the preparation of flax for weaving into linen. The Rotherham feoffees had also built a workhouse by 1659, and here the poor made 'fustions and other commodityes called Manchester ware'. Earlier in the century, sometime during the reign of James I, the West Riding JPs had established a workhouse at Wortley 'for the seting of poor children on work ... in Garsey Kniting weving fustion Clothing or sume other good work.' A jersey knitter was appointed as master, but so far no other seventeenth-century record of this enterprise has come to light.

The necessity of providing for the poor is apparent from a document that was drawn up on 2 January 1615/16 by twenty-four Sheffield men. They had been asked to conduct a census so that Gilbert, seventh Earl of Shrewsbury, would have reliable information upon which to base his proposed charity. This was a time of distress in many English towns, with great numbers living at or below the poverty level. Of the 2,207 people living within the township (as distinct from the entire parish) of Sheffield, 725 were said to be 'not able to live without the charity of their neighbours. These are all begging poore.' They amounted to 32.85 per cent of the population, a figure that accords with estimates made of the proportion of paupers in other contemporary towns. The remaining 1,482 people consisted of householders, children and servants (wives are presumably included in this total figure, but the document is ambiguous), with an average household size of 4.7 people. Of these, 100 householders were able to pay the poor rates; 'These (though the best sorte) are but poor artificers; among them is not one which can keep a teame on his own land, and not above tenn who have grounds of their own that keepe a cow.' The other 160 householders were unable to assist the poor and paid no rates; 'These are such (though they beg not) are not able to abide the storme of one fortnight's sickness, but would be thereby driven to beggary.' Furthermore, most of the servants or children were 'such as live of small wages, and are constrained to worke sore, to provide them necessaries.' There may have been an element of special pleading in all this, with an eye to obtaining a substantial charity, but nevertheless the picture of a struggle against poverty is a very real one.

All over the country, communities were still vulnerable to the devastating effects of harvest failure and epidemic disease. Little demographic research has as yet been undertaken in South Yorkshire, but the signs are that the county was affected by dearth during the last two decades of the sixteenth century. The number of burials at Hatfield was abnormally high in 1592, and the number of deaths at Laughton reached a new peak in 1597. These were years of crisis in many parts of the country. At Sheffield, a record number of 178 deaths was recorded in 1592, but five years later no less than 253 people were buried there. Epidemics were a recurrent hazard that were not necessarily linked to the effects of starvation. The worst outbreak of disease killed hundreds of people in Doncaster in the early 1580s. Between September 1582 and December 1583 the parish registers record the burials of 747 people with the letter 'P' against their names to denote bubonic plague. The town suffered milder attacks on several other occasions up to 1645, but 'plague' was a general term that was used to describe a variety of diseases. The authorities always attempted to confine the epidemic to the infected areas. In 1665, for instance, the justices of the peace of West Riding banned carriers from trading with London and ordered 'watch and ward' to be set up at the various points of entry to the county.

25 Schools

Economic hardship was often mitigated by charity. Professor W.K. Jordan has shown that Yorkshire people were generous in their charitable bequests and that, compared with the country as a whole, schools received a high proportion of the endowments. Before the Reformation a fifth of the recorded bequests went to the schools; by the Elizabethan and Stuart period this share had almost doubled. Tickhill school was founded in 1349 by the wife of a local gentleman, and that at Penistone was founded in 1392 by the lord of the manor, Thomas Clarel, but most schools had a shadowy existence during their early years and it is difficult to judge whether there was any continuity. Grammar schools existed in Doncaster and Sheffield during the early years of the reign of Elizabeth, and the feoffees' school was established in Ecclesfield by 1573. Several others had no doubt been founded by this time, but endowments were often small and the number of pupils few. A school was built on waste ground to the north of the churchyard at Worsbrough in 1560, but it was not until John Rayney made a substantial bequest in 1632 that the master was sufficiently provided for, in order to teach 'learning, writing, cyphering [and] the grounds of religion.' The building that survives may well date from that time.

The traditional position of the school was close by the church. At Harthill and at Felkirk (just north of the county boundary) the schools were actually built inside the churchyard, and no doubt because of similar proximity the schoolboys of Cawthorne were able to lock a bride inside the church in 1618 when she refused to pay them the sixpence that was customary upon such occasions. The oldest surviving school in the county is the delightful building opposite the north side of the church at Laughton, which was erected sometime between 1610 and 1619 on land given by Anthony Eyre and Edmund Laughton. More opportunities for schooling were available during this period than historians once realised.

68

The village school at Laughton en le Morthen was erected during the second decade of the seventeenth century. The oldest surviving school building in the county, it stands (as was usual) close to the church.

Bequests to schools are recorded at Hatfield (1619), Bolsterstone (1622), Kirk Sandall (1616), Fishlake (1641), Barnsley (1646), Wath (1647) and Stannington (1653), and no doubt there were schools within reach of most villages. Nevertheless, it is true that the endowments were often insufficient to guarantee a school's future, and that private schools usually lasted only until the death, retirement, or change of occupation or locality of the master.

26   Churches and the Reformation

Internal changes   The founders of these schools were motivated by Protestant, and sometimes by Puritan beliefs. The Reformation represented a major change from the past and affected every community in the country. Its immediate effect was to bring to an end the great Perpendicular phase of church building and restoration. Most of the ancient churches of South Yorkshire retain the external appearance that they had acquired by or during the reign of Henry VIII, but internally all is changed. Once, all was a blaze of colour, with wall paintings, stained glass windows and gilded images of the saints. At the Reformation the images were destroyed, the walls were covered with whitewash, sentences from the Scriptures replaced the pictures of saints and angels, and the royal arms were hung over the chancel arch in place of a painting of the Day of Judgment. Other changes of liturgy and belief involve the abandonment of the Easter sepulchres and of the sedilia and piscina used by the priests in the chancel, and the banning of all processions, even (for a time) the Rogationtide beating of the parish bounds.

The course of the Reformation was chronicled by Robert Parkyn, the conservative curate of Adwick le Street. Parkyn was essentially a medievalist in outlook, a man involved in mystical studies in the Richard Rolle tradition. He seldom left South Yorkshire but had read most of the important theological works of his day and had himself written a metrical *Life of Christ*. It appears from his account that although he and his fellow clerics detested the changes, most of them complied readily with the government decrees. No resistance movement was formed in his neighbourhood. Indeed, at Rotherham there was such haste to conform that the churchwardens paid for hand-written copies of the Edwardian service-books until such time as printed copies were available. Parkyn wrote that, only a few weeks after the government decree, 'in the monethe of Decembre [1550] all allters of stoyne was taken away...furthe of the churches and chappels from Trentt northewardes and a table of woode sett in the qweare.' And whereas most people had once stood in the nave, with 'the weak to the wall', it became increasingly the fashion to install private pews. The splendid examples at Sprotbrough have carved figures at each end and can be dated to the 1550s. Eventually, the seating plans formalised the social structure of the community, with the leading figures at the front, the ordinary farmers and craftsmen behind them, and the labourers at the rear.

Reaction to all this came during the reign of Queen Mary, and afterwards there was less haste to comply with government orders. The accounts of the Capital Burgesses show that the stone altars were not removed from Sheffield church until 1560, that a plain communion table was not installed until 1566 and that the churchyard cross was not removed until 1570. Furthermore, in the neighbouring parish of Ecclesfield it was not until 1569 that the stone altars were replaced by a wooden communion table, that the great crucifix above the rood-screen was taken down, images of the saints destroyed, the 'passion clothes' sold, and a new bible was purchased.

The church courts   It is difficult to gauge the reactions of ordinary people to these changes. The Church played a very important role in their lives, yet their beliefs have been apty described as a mundane utilitariansim. Priests were often regarded as intermediaries with the supernatural in much the same way as were the wise-men and wise-women, the village conjurors. Thus, at Penistone in 1598 Jasper Walshaw was charged with 'abusing the Churchwardens sayinge that it [had] beene good that wise men had been in Office for they were fooles neyther will he obey them in any respecte.' Mr P. Tyler has shown that between 1567 and 1640 the ecclesiastical courts at York presented 117 people on charges of witchcraft. However, only four or five of these cases involved any suspicion of formal cursing or black witchcraft. Those charged were not regarded as heretics and were treated leniently with small fines and penances. Nevertheless, witch beliefs were undoubtedly more widespread than the surviving references suggest and also of long continuance. Even in the mid-nineteenth century the wise-man of High Green had a considerable local reputation as a recoverer of stolen goods. Medieval documentation is rare, but it is recorded that in 1465 William Byg alias Lech was practising as a magician in Wombwell, and that in 1481 John Parkyn was presented as a wizard in Handsworth. The surviving ecclesiastical court books date from 1598, when two women from Barnby Dun and two others from Darfield were charged with witchcraft, a woman from Campsall and two people from Rotherham were suspected of sorcery, and a Bolton upon Dearne woman was alleged to have been a charmer. Furthermore, William Taylor of Darton was said to have sent to a reputed wise-woman at Darfield 'to knowe a remedy for his sicknes and her resolucon was that he was bewitched.' Mr K. Thomas and Dr A. MacFarlane have shown that the great majority of witchcraft accusations throughout the country were directed against a pauper by someone who had previously refused charity to that person. The great increase in the number of the Elizabethan and Stuart poor created the tensions that gave rise to witch-beliefs.

The ecclesiastical courts were responsible not only for ensuring attendance at church and conformity of religious beliefs, but for matters of social discipline. The normal penalty for infringing the moral code was public penance in the church. The guilty person had to stand before the congregation draped in a white sheet and carrying a white wand. He or she had to confess to his or her sins and ask for communal prayers for forgiveness. In a society whose whole structure of thought was dominated by religion, this could be a very powerful weapon, for the failure to perform this act brought the threat of excommunication. However, most offenders were treated leniently, for the authorities did not feel threatened by minor misdemeanours. Typical of the charges in 1598 were that William Mowsleye of Cantley spread dung on a Sunday, that three Doncaster men abused the churchwardens 'in vile speches in the Churche', and that Elizabeth Scales of Hooton Roberts had called her mother a witch. Elizabeth Scruton of the parish of Silkstone had achieved sufficient notoriety to be described as a blasphemer of God's holy word, a common scold, a curser, a swearer, a banner and a brawler, and in 1636 Gilbert Waddilove of Thurnscoe was charged with being a common alehouse haunter and with abusing the churchwardens, saying that he would pay his church-rates when the devil was blind.

The Puritans   The Puritan party within the Church of England did not make much headway in South Yorkshire during the Elizabethan period. In 1604 only three of the sixty parishes of the deanery of Doncaster had ministers who were ardent puritans, though another parson shared some of their beliefs, and thirteen others were 'seeming weary of the ceremonies'. In the south-east of the county the prospects of establishing a puritan form of worship seemed so poor that several families joined their friends from the Scrooby area, just across the county boundary, in emigrating to America. One of those who sailed on the Mayflower was William Bradford of Austerfield, who was then 30 years old. He became Governor of Plymouth Colony in April 1621 and remained in that office, except for a five year period, until his death in 1657.

During the third decade of the seventeenth century the puritans grew both in numbers and influence, particularly in the western parts of the county. They attracted the support of many of the leading townsmen and some of the country gentry. In 1622 for instance, Thomas Cutler endowed £300 for the maintenance of 'a zealous preacher' at Stainborough. There was a growing need for such chapels in the west, where the ancient parishes were too large for the ministers to serve adequately. In 1627 Godfrey Bosville of Gunthwaite Hall built a chapel at Denby and installed a Puritan curate, and two years later Stephen Bright of Carbrook and William

69

St James's, Midhope, was originally a chapel-of-ease in the enormous parish of Ecclesfield. Godfrey Bosville, the lord of the manor, rebuilt it in 1705, using some of the existing walls. Externally, it retains much of its medieval appearance, and internally it is still furnished as in Bosville's time.

Spencer of Attercliffe began work on a chapel at Attercliffe. The Bosvilles held the right to appoint vicars at Penistone, and the right to appoint at Sheffield belonged to another puritan family, the Jessops of Broom Hall, so there were no unseemly disputes over dues. Thomas Toller, the vicar of Sheffield from 1598 to 1635 was one of the most extreme puritans.

In 1635 Archbishop Neile ordered a counter-attack upon the puritans within the diocese of York. Following a policy similar to that of William Laud, Archbishop of Canterbury, he used the annual church visitations to 'beautify' the churches and to install communion tables and rails. Toller was forced to resign, and other vicars were made to conform. At Laughton, for instance, the vicar was presented in 1636 for not wearing the surplice, not teaching the catechism, and for not declaring holy days and fasting days; the following year a Laudian communion table and rails were placed within the chancel and services reverted to the official form. Neile's victory appeared complete, and in 1638 he reported to Charles I that many of the puritan clergy of South Yorkshire were emigrating to America.

27 The Civil War

This dispute over religion came to a head in the Civil War, when religious and political loyalties were closely related. The man most associated with Charles's policies during the 1630s was Sir Thomas Wentworth, the Earl of Strafford, who took his title from the name of the wapentake. His family were ancient gentry in South Yorkshire and had acquired their surname from their place of residence. Thomas's father, Sir William Wentworth, had been sheriff of Yorkshire in 1601-2 and had been created a baronet in 1611. He was the richest gentleman in Yorkshire, with an estate worth £6,000 per annum. Thomas's career was of national rather than local importance, but for a time he lived in great style at Wentworth Woodhouse, with a household of 64 persons, including 49 servants. A number of neighbouring gentlemen, such as Thomas Edmunds of Worsbrough, Richard Elmhirst of Houndhill, Robert Rockley of Rockley, and Sir Richard Scott of Barnes Hall, served as deputies when he was Lord President of the Council of the North and Lord Deputy of Ireland. But personal ties did not always guarantee complete loyalty, for after Strafford's execution in 1641, his brother-in-law, Sir Edward Rhodes of Great Houghton, fought on the side of parliament.

On the outbreak of civil war in 1642 opinion in Yorkshire was divided. Dr J.T.Cliffe has shown that 242 gentry families supported the royalist cause, 128 supported parliament, 69 families were either divided in their allegiances or changed sides during the war, and 240 were neutral. Loyalties cannot be explained in economic terms, for there were no fundamental differences in the wealth of royalist and parliamentarian families. On balance, opposition to the crown was more closely associated with growing prosperity than with economic decline, but on the other hand many successful landowners were fervent royalists. In South Yorkshire a majority of influential people supported the parliamentary cause, but there were some wealthy and powerful men arranged against them.

The leading royalists included Sir Edward Osborne of Thorpe Salvin, who had been Vice-President of the Council of the North from 1633 to 1641, Sir Francis Wortley, who organised a garrison at Tankersley, Sir John Reresby of Thrybergh, several of Strafford's former deputies, and Gervase Cutler of Stainborough, who contributed £1,000 to the royalist cause despite his attachment to the puritan form of religion. Cutler was killed during the war and his entire estate was plundered. The parliamentary gentry included Jessop of Broom Hall, Bright of Carbrook and Spencer of Attercliffe, each of whom lived in the parish of Sheffield; and further north, in the parish of Penistone, Godfrey Bosville of Gunthwaite, Adam Eyre of Hazlehead, William Rich of Bullhouse, and the Wordsworths of Water Hall. The townspeople of South Yorkshire were also firm supporters of Parliament. In previous troubles Sheffield had been loyal to the crown, but there was no longer a resident lord to command obedience. In 1642, John, the son of Stephen Bright, raised a local force and with the aid of Sir John Gell's Derbyshire troops took Sheffield castle without a fight. By the end of the year Parliament had the upper hand in South Yorkshire.

In the spring of 1643 the Earl of Newcastle's royalist troops launched a counter-attack. The parliamentarians withdrew rather than fight against superior numbers, and the only local battle that has been recorded during this period was a royalist victory on Tankersley Moor, where (according to Newcastle's wife) 'many were slain and some taken prisoners'. The royalists re-occupied the castle at Sheffield and evicted the puritan ministers before marching onto Rotherham, where the townsmen were heavily fined for their opposition. John Shaw, the puritan vicar, escaped arrest by hiding in the steeple before fleeing to Manchester. Doncaster and Tickhill were also taken without much trouble.

The county remained under royalist control for more than a year, during which time they requisitioned the local ironworks in order to cast cannon. The turning point came in July 1644 with Cromwell's famous victory at Marston Moor in North Yorkshire. By the 23rd of July parliamentary troops had re-occupied Doncaster and a party under Lt-Col John Lilburne took Tickhill castle with hardly a fight. Rotherham was then taken with some difficulty by about a thousand infantry and an unspecified number of horsemen under the command of Maj-Gen Crawford, and plans were laid for an assault upon Sheffield. John Bright was sent to York to fetch heavy artillery, and the castle was beseiged with the enthusiastic support of the townsfolk. Local miners were unable to tunnel through the rock to drain the moat, so no attack could be made until the local forges had produced sufficient cannon balls and Bright had arrived with large cannon. His reinforcements came on August 9th and the walls were soon breached. The commander, Major Beaumont, surrendered upon receiving a promise of safe conduct, but 30 of his soldiers fought on. Two days later they came out drunk and brawling and the fight was over.

There were minor skirmishes near the seats of the royalist gentry, for example at Houndhill, where Richard Elmhirst had garrisoned his house with 40 soldiers, but the royalist cause soon collapsed completely. Its leading supporters were punished severely. Sir Francis Wortley, for instance, spent many years in prison, and Sir John Reresby died in 1646 with debts amounting to £1,200, his park stripped of its timber, its pales broken and its deer removed. All over the county royalist vicars were replaced by puritan preachers, and though the damage done has been greaty exaggerated, many churches were refashioned internally.

With the final victory of Parliament an era came to an end. The Reformation had swept away the monasteries and chantries and had altered the internal appearance of the churches and the form of the services. Now it was the turn of that other great symbol of the medieval age, the castle. Many of these strongholds had been garrisoned by royalist forces up and down the country, and the parliamentarians were determined that they would not be used in this way again. Thus, in 1648 the castles at Sheffield and Tickhill were dismantled, and Conisbrough survived only because it was already in decay and had not been used in the recent wars.

Epilogue

In the attractive little village of Warmsworth, which lies tucked away from
the hustle and bustle of two major roads, stands a curious bell tower of
unknown date. It was there in 1726 but opinions as to how much older it is
vary considerably. Built on the rector's land just outside the gates of the
hall, it announced the services which were held in the church half a mile
away. We know from documentary evidence that Warmsworth had a
priest, and therefore presumably a church, in the twelfth century and that
the medieval building was replaced by a new structure on the same site in
the nineteenth century. The building was abandoned when a modern
church was erected at a more convenient place in 1941, and during the
winter of 1977-8 the chance arose to excavate the foundations.

W.G.Hoskins has written that, 'A church standing far from its
parishioners is as provocative a start as the discovery of the body at the
outset of a detective story.' The puzzle is complicated by the fact that
Warmsworth church stood right on the parish boundary, where the
medieval lordship known as the soke of Doncaster had been carved from
the great territory that formed the fee of Conisbrough by the beginning of
the eleventh century and possibly long before. Why was it there?

We still do not know. The excavations revealed the foundations of the
original, simple church on top of an earlier burial ground. Norman
sculptured stones were found and later alterations distinguished. The dig
inspired fresh documentary research into the history of the church and the
community which it served, and a great deal has been learnt about
Warmsworth in the Middle Ages. But the reason for the strange choice of
site remains a matter for speculation. One obvious suggestion is that
perhaps the village has been moved from an earlier position nearer the
church. A careful analysis of a map of 1726 suggests that this may have
happened, for the village has such a regular arrangement that it must have
been deliberately planned. Villages in other parts of Yorkshire were
rebuilt on regular lines after the Norman conquest; perhaps some of our
rural settlements, as well as our towns, were laid out anew? Warmsworth
had acquired its present plan, with open fields stretching right to the
parish boundaries by the early fourteenth century, but there are no clues as
to the whereabouts of an earlier settlement, and now that the area is covered
with modern housing there is little chance that any will be found. Some of
the secrets of the historical landscape will remain for ever locked from us.

Nevertheless, the combined techniques of archaeology, history, historical geography and various other specialisms will undoubtedly deepen further our understanding of the way that South Yorkshire has been moulded by its past. There are also welcome signs of increasing interest in the preservation of the county's archaeological features and its ancient buildings. The cost of preservation is often prohibitive when other deserving projects are in need of funds, but the time has now come to question whether or not what is being done in the name of progress is invariably better than the old. Each case needs to be examined on its merits, and this book will have served its purpose if it has increased its reader's interest in the way that his or her surroundings have been shaped by its history.

70

This curious bell tower of unknown date stands on the parson's land in the village of Warmsworth just beyond the grounds of the hall. It announced the services that were held in the church half a mile away. The church occupied a lonely position right on the parish boundary.

Glossary

Advowson: right to appoint a rector or vicar

Agger: raised stretch of Roman road

Anglo-Scandinavian: belonging to the Angles and Vikings of the pre-Norman period

Ashlar: stone cut to a smooth finish

Assart: field cleared from the waste

Aula: term used in Domesday Book for an Anglo-Scandinavian hall

Ball-flower: early-fourteenth century decoration with three petals enclosing a ball

Berewick: dependent farm

Bierlow: Viking term for a township

Boon-work: one of a peasant's obligations to his lord

Bressumer: beam between the base and the superstructure of a timber-framed building

Burgage plot: long, narrow piece of property behind the house of an urban freeman

Burh: Anglo-Saxon fort

Carucate: term used in Domesday Book for a taxable unit of about 120 acres

Celtic: belonging to the native British people

Chancel: eastern part of a church, containing the altar

Chantry: private chapel, usually attached to or inside a church

Chapelry: area served by a chapel, which did not have the full rights of a parish church

Clerestory: upper wall of the nave of a chapel, containing a range of windows

Demesne: land within a manor held personally by the lord

Fee: large, medieval lordship

Feoffees: trustees responsible for a charity

Glebe terrier: list of property belonging to a church

Herringbone walling: stones laid diagonally in alternate courses to form a zig-zag pattern

Honour: large, medieval lordship

Intersected tracery: early-fourteenth century window decoration, with mullions crossing each other in upper part

King-post: post which rests on a tie-beam and supports the ridge-pole of a roof

Long-and-short work: Anglo-Saxon quoins consisting of stones placed with the long sides alternately upright and horizontal

Lancet: slender thirteenth-century window with pointed arch

Maison Dieu: small religious hospital

Minster: missionary centre, or mother church

Mullion: upright, usually of stone, dividing a window into two or more 'lights'

Ogee arch: fourteenth-century arch curving to a point

Pilaster: thin buttress, especially of the Norman period

Piscina: basin for washing Mass vessels

Porticus: side-chapel of an Anglo-Saxon church

Purlin: horizontal beam for supporting rafters

Quo Warranto enquiries: late-thirteenth century royal investigation into property rights

Quoins: dressed stones at the angles of a building

Romano-British: Romans and native British people under Roman rule

Rood loft: gallery above the screen and Crucifix dividing the chancel from the nave

Sedilia: seats for priests on south side of a chancel

Slitting mill: works where iron was split into bars or rods

Soke: large, medieval lordship

Sokemen: term used in Domesday Book to describe a class of freemen

Staithe: wharf

Tenters: frames on which cloth was stretched and dried

Tie-beam: beam connecting the uprights of a timber-framed building

Township: smallest unit of medieval government, often a sub-division of a parish

Turbary: right to dig peat

Wall-plate: horizontal post supporting the base of the rafters on top of the wall

Wapentake: Danish sub-division of a county, equivalent to the Anglo-Saxon hundred

Zig-Zag decoration: Norman artistic style

Bibliography

Books and Pamphlets

Addy, S.O., *The Evolution of the English House,* 1910

Ambler, L., *Old Halls and Manor Houses of Yorkshire,* 1913

Beresford, M.W., *New Towns of the Middle Ages,* 1967

Beresford, M.W., and Hurst, J.C., *Deserted Medieval Villages,* 1971

Beswick, P., *Bishops' House* (Sheffield City Museum Information Sheet 16), 1976

Cameron, K. (ed), *Place-Name Evidence for the Anglo-Saxon Invasion and Scandinavian Settlements,* 1975

Clayton, A.K., *Hoyland Nether,* 1974

Clay, J.W. (ed), *Yorkshire Church Notes, 1619-1631 by Roger Dodsworth,* Yorkshire Archaeological Society Record Series, XXXIV, 1904

Cliffe, J.T., *The Yorkshire Gentry from the Reformation to the Civil War,* 1969

Darby, H.C., and Maxwell, I.S. (eds), *Domesday Geography of Northern England,* 1962

Dickens, A.G., *Lollards and Protestants in the Diocese of York, 1509-58,* 1959

Dobson, R.B., and Taylor, J., *Rymes of Robyn Hood,* 1976

Eastwood, J., *History of the Parish of Ecclesfield,* 1862

Elmhirst, E., *Peculiar Inheritance,* 1951

Finucane, R.C., *Miracles and Pilgrims: Popular Beliefs in Medieval England,* 1977

Girouard, M., *Robert Smythson and the Architecture of the Elizabethan Era,* 1966

Graham, R., and Gilyard-Beer, R., *Monk Bretton Priory* (Department of the Environment guide), 1966

Guest, J., *Historic Notices of Rotherham,* 1879

Hall, T.W., *Descriptive Catalogues...* (several volumes of transcribed deeds, charters, wills, manorial rolls, etc. relating to Sheffield and other parts of South Yorkshire, 1913-39)

Hatfield, C.W., *Historic Notices of Doncaster,* 3 vols, 1866-70

Hey, D., *The Village of Ecclesfield,* 1968

Hey, D., *Rural Metalworkers of the Sheffield Region,* 1972

Holland, D., *Bawtry and the Idle River Trade,* 1976

Holland, D., (ed), *History in Laughton en le Morthen,* 1969

Hunter, J., *Hallamshire*, 1819

Hunter J., *South Yorkshire: the History of Topography of the Deanery of Doncaster*, 2 vols, 1828-31

Innocent, C.F., *Development of English Building Construction*, 1916

Jackson, J.E., *History of the Ruined Church of St. Mary Magdalene*, 1853

Jackson, J.E., *History of St George's Church, Doncaster*, 1855

Kenworthy, J., *History of Stocksbridge and District*, 1927

Jordan, W.K., *The Charities of Rural England, 1480-1660*, 1961

Keble- Martin, W., *A History of the Ancient Parish of Wath-upon-Dearne*, 1920

Knowles, D., and Hadcock, R.N., *Medieval Religious Houses: England and Wales*, 1953

Leader, R.E., *History of the Cutlers Company in Hallamshire*, 2 vols, 1905-6

Lloyd, G.I.H., *The Cutlery Trades*, 1913

Magilton, J.R., *The Doncaster District: an Archaeological Survey*, 1977

Margary, I.D., *Roman Roads in Britain*, 1967

May, T., *The Roman Forts of Templeborough*, 1922

Le Patourel, H.E.J., *The Moated Sites of Yorkshire*, 1973

Pevsner, N., *The Buildings of England: Yorkshire, The West Riding*, 1959

Ruston, A., and Witney, D., *Hooton Pagnell: the Agricultural Evolution of a Yorkshire Village*, 1934

Skaife, R.H., *Domesday Book of Yorkshire*, 1896

Smith, A.H. (ed), *The Place-Names of the West Riding of Yorkshire*, parts 1 and 2, 1961

Smith, L.T., *The Itinerary of John Leland*, vol. 1, 1964

Smith, R.B., *Land and Politics in the England of Henry VIII: the West Riding of Yorkshire, 1530-1546*, 1970

Taylor, H.M. and J., *Anglo-Saxon Architecture*, 2 vols, 1965

Thompson, A.H., *Roche Abbey* (Department of the Environment guide), 1954

Thompson, A.H., and Clay, C.T. (eds), *Fasti Parochiales*, vols 1 and 2, 1933 and 1943

Thompson, M.W., *Conisbrough Castle* (Department of the Environment guide), 1959

Timson, R.T. (ed), *The Cartulary of Blyth Priory*, vol. 1, 1973

Tomlinson, J., *Doncaster from the Roman Occupation to the Present Time*, 1887

Tomlinson, J., *The Level of Hatfield Chase and Parts Adjacent*, 1882

Walton, M., *Sheffield: its Story and Achievement*, 1948

Wilkinson, J., *Worsbrough: its Historical Associations and Rural Attractions*, 1872

Yorkshire Archaeological and Topographical Association, *The Returns of the Poll Tax for the West Riding of Yorkshire, 1379*, 1882

Articles

Armstrong, A.L., 'Sheffield Castle', *Trans Hunter Archaeol Soc*, IV, pt 1, 1930

Beresford, M.W., 'Glebe Terriers and Open Field Yorkshire', *Yorks Archaeol Journal*, 37, 1950

Buckland, P.C., 'A Roman-British Pottery Kiln Site at Branton near Doncaster', *Yorks Archaeol Journal*, 48, 1976

Butcher, L.H., 'Archaeological Remains on the Wharncliffe-Greno-Upland, South Yorkshire', *Trans Hunter Archaeol Soc VII, pt 1, 1957*

Cox, B., 'The Significance of the Distribution of English Place-Names in *Ham* in the Midlands and East Anglia', *Journal of the English Place Name Soc* 5, 1973

Cregeen, S.M., 'Kilns 22-25 and Iron Smelting Furnace 1 (Cantley)', *Yorks Archaeol Journal*, 39, 1956

Crossley, D., and Ashurst, D., 'Excavations at Rockley Smithies, a Water-Powered Bloomery of the Sixteenth and Seventeenth Centuries', *Post-Medieval Archaeology*, 2, 1968

Curtis, E., 'Sheffield in the Fourteenth Century', *Trans Hunter Archaeol Soc* 1, pt 1, 1914

Davies, G.T., 'St. Peter's Church, Conisbrough: A Preliminary Note on Its Date', in D. Holland, ed, *Sprotbrough in History*, pt 2, 1969

Dickens, A.G., 'Robert Parkyn's Narrative of the Reformation', *English Historical Review*, LXII, 1947

Gaunt, G.D., 'The Artificial Nature of the River Don North of Thorne, Yorkshire', *Yorks Archaeol Journal*, 47, 1975

Gilmour, E.F., 'The Roman Excavations at Cantley Housing Estate', *Yorks Archaeol Journal*, 38, 1955, and 39, 1956

Green, D., 'Moat Hall, Braithwell', *Trans Hunter Archaeol Soc*, V, pt 5, 1942

Harvey, J.C., 'Common Field and Enclosure in the Lower Dearne Valley', *Yorks Archaeol Journal*, 46, 1974

Hey, D., 'The Parks at Tankersley and Wortley', *Yorks Archaeol Journal*, 47, 1975

Hopkinson, G.G., 'The Development of the South Yorkshire and North Derbyshire Coalfield, 1500-1775', *Trans Hunter Archaeol Soc*, VII, pt 6, 1957

Hopkinson, G.G., 'The Charcoal Iron Industry in the Sheffield Region, 1500-1775', *Trans Hunter Archaeol Soc*, VIII, pt 3, 1961

Innocent, C.F., 'The Field system of Wightwizle', *Trans Hunter Archaeol Soc*, 11, pt 3, 1922

Jensen, G.F., 'Place-Names and Settlement History: a Review with a Select Bibliography of Works Mostly Published Since 1960', *Northern History*, XIII, 1977

Jolliffe, J.E.A., 'Northumbrian Institutions', *English Historical Review,* XLI, 1926

Jones, G.R.J., 'Early Territorial Organisation in Gwynedd and Elmet', *Northern History,* X, 1975

Mott, R.A., 'The Water Mills of Beauchief Abbey', *Trans Hunter Archaeol Soc,* IX, pt 4, 1969

Northend, W.F., 'The Hall in the Ponds', *Trans Hunter Archaeol Soc,* VII, pt 1, 1951

Preston, F.L., 'A Field Survey of the 'Roman Rig' Dyke in South-West Yorkshire', *Trans Hunter Archaeol Soc,* VI, pt 5, 1949, and VI, pt 6, 1950

Revill, S., 'King Edwin and the Battle of Heathfield', *Trans Thoroton Soc,* LXXIX, 1975

Riley, D.N., *Yorks Archaeol Journal,* 45, 1973; 48, 1976; 49, 1977. Three articles on air reconnaissance in Yorkshire.

Thomas, A.H., 'Some Hallamshire Rolls of the Fifteenth Century', *Trans Hunter Archaeol Soc,* 11, pt 1, 1920; pt, 1921; pt 3, 1922

Tyler, P., 'The Church Courts at York and Witchcraft Prosecutions, 1567-1640', *Northern History,* IV, 1969

Whiting, C.E., 'Excavations at Stancil, 1938-9', *Yorks Archaeol Journal,* 35, 1941

Wigfull, J.R., 'Broom Hall, Sheffield', *Trans Hunter Archaeol Soc* IV, pt 2, 1932

The Yorkshire Archaeological Register, *Yorks Archaeol Journal,* annually.

Documentary Sources

Sheffield Central Library Archives Department: charters, deeds, surveys, rentals, manorial rolls, maps and plans in various collections.

Borthwick Institute of Historical Research, York: wills and inventories, archbishops' registers, tithe awards, ecclesiastical court records.

Public Record Office, London: Exchequer, Chancery, Duchy of Lancaster and War Office records.

British Library, London: Lansdowne and Additional manuscripts.

Doncaster Metropolitan Borough Record Office: corporation records.

West Yorks County Record Office: quarter session records.

Lichfield Joint Record Office: wills and inventories for parts of the county formerly within Derbyshire.

The transcripts of Crown-copyright material appear by permission of the Controller of Her Majesty's Stationery Office.

Index

Rotherham, Archbishop, 57, 105
Rough Birchworth, 12, 22, 45, 73
Royston, 94, 95, 99, 136

St Ellen chapels, 75, 84-5
Salt trade, 8, 61-3
Saltersbrook, 61, 62, 65, 85
Sandford family, 93, 114, 133
Savage family, 93
Saxton, Christopher, 62, 81, 85
Scawsby, 24, 62, 66, 77, 127, 136
Schools, 54, 137, 139, 140, 141-2, 143
Scythe-making, 122-3, 134
Shafton, 121, 126
Sheaf, River, 21, 27, 29, 55, 99
Sheffield, 7, 8, 11, 12, 18, 19, 21, 23, 24,
    26, 27, 28, 29, 35, 42, 46, 53, 54-5, 57,
    61, 63, 64, 65, 70, 72, 80, 82, 93, 95, 96,
    100, 102, 105, 107, 108, 111, 112, 114,
    117, 120, 121, 122, 124, 131, 132, 133,
    137, 138, 139, 140, 141, 142, 144, 146
Shiregreen, 28, 108
Shore Hall farm, 110
Shrewsbury, Earls of, 60, 82, 96, 97, 113,
    114, 120, 121, 133, 139, 140
Silkstone, 8, 33, 57, 58, 62, 90, 94, 96, 102
    103, 118, 121, 145
Skellow, 44
Skinthorpe, 77
Snowden Hill, 73, 83
Spott, Wulfric, 30, 52
Sprotbrough, 19, 23, 35, 77, 91, 92, 93,
    96, 103, 114, 124, 143
Stainborough, 23, 33, 73, 101, 114, 145,
    147
Staincross wapentake, 25, 32, 33, 42, 70,
    113
Stainforth, 30, 66, 71, 132
Stainton, 22
Stairfoot, 64, 73
Stanage Pole, 27, 61, 64
Stancil, 18, 48, 114, 127
Stannington, 18, 73, 143
Strafford Sands, 17, 20, 32, 44
Strafforth and Tickhill wapentake, 17,
    25, 26, 113
Strelley family, 114, 118
Swaithe Hall, 108, 111
Swinton, 113, 121
Sykehouse, 26, 75, 129, 130, 132

Tankersley, 8, 22, 78-82, 117, 120, 121,
    133, 147, 148
Tanning, 124-5
Templeborough, 13, 14, 17, 18, 20, 21,
    28, 85, 101
Textiles, 59, 103, 110, 123-4, 128, 140
Thorne, 10, 30, 32, 44, 60, 71, 75, 76, 93,
    117, 124, 130

Thorpe in Balne, 24, 26, 78-80
Thorpe Hesley, 62, 63, 85, 114
Thorpe Salvin, 15, 40, 89, 91, 114, 127,
    128, 133-4, 147
Throapham, 18, 40, 41, 84
Thrybergh, 35, 82, 86, 93, 94, 117, 147
Thundercliffe Grange, 118, 121
Thurcroft, 17, 41, 75
Thurgoland, 33, 126
Thurlstone, 24, 62, 73, 115
Thurnscoe, 18, 77, 85, 121, 145
Tickhill, 17, 18, 30, 33, 41, 42, 44, 46,
    47-52, 53, 58, 64, 65, 71, 72, 91, 92, 93,
    94, 96, 98, 104, 113, 114, 127, 132, 136,
    141, 148
Tilli, Ote de, 70, 86
Tilts, 52, 78
Todwick, 34, 37, 95, 99
Toller, Thomas, 146
Torne, River, 14, 129
Treeton, 34, 85, 96
Tudworth, 30, 130
Turf, 60, 75, 76, 128

Vermuyden, Cornelius, 9, 14, 128-9
Village markets, 65-71

Wadsley, 22, 74, 82, 118, 131
Wadworth, 19, 37, 87, 91, 103, 117
Wales, 20, 30, 40, 87, 108, 121
Waltheof, Earl, 29, 41, 42, 47, 54
Wapentakes, 17, 25, 26, 33, 42, 70, 113
Wardsend, 121, 125
Warenne, Earls of, 32, 45, 46, 71, 81, 86
Warmsworth, 4, 24, 32, 75, 117, 124,
    149, 150
Wath upon Dearne, 17, 22, 25, 61, 66,
    69, 87, 91, 94, 96, 143
Wentworth, 18, 47, 75, 94, 102, 114, 117,
    121, 147
Wentworth family, 114, 126, 129, 147
West Thorpe, 16, 40
Wharncliffe, 19, 70, 81, 115-16
Wheatley, 14, 15, 18, 34, 52
Whiston, 17, 25, 29, 30, 108-10, 120, 121
Whitley, 124, 134
Wickersley, 33
Wigtwizzle, 72, 73, 134-5
Widthorpe, 78, 127
Wilsic, 30, 48
Wirral, family, 95, 114, 127
Wincobank, 7, 12, 13, 28, 29
Wombwell, 11, 61, 71, 144
Worsbrough, 23, 86, 96, 108, 121, 126,
    134, 136, 139, 142, 147
Wortley, 62, 66, 70, 81, 82, 114, 115, 116,
    117, 118, 140
Wortley family, 81, 85, 114, 115-17, 118,
    121, 126, 147, 148